The facebook™ datebook

FOR MEN

Written by Flyness

**THE ULTIMATE REFERENCE GUIDE
FOR MEETING WOMEN ON FACEBOOK!**

THANKS :

Thanks to The Princess, Miss Fray, Leon, Phil, my fellow macks, and everyone who's supported my book series, "From MySpace To My Place" which continues to do well! If you liked those books, you'll LOVE this one!

There was a lot of time and effort that went into putting this book together. The process took many hours over the course of many weeks. That means that this information has value and your friends, neighbors, and co-workers may want to share it. The price of this book is very small, compared to the value you are getting from it. So if your friends like the concept of the book, please encourage them to purchase their own copy from **www.TheFacebookDatebook.com.**

Make sure you follow @Flyness on Twitter and check out his other titles at www.MySpaceToMyPlace.com!

The Facebook Datebook, by Flyness
Flyness Publishing

ISBN: 978-0-578-04402-6

Table of Contents

Introduction

It's been a minute everyone, but I'm back! And in case you're wondering what I'm talking about, I am *Your Royal Flyness*, the author that "literally" brought you *From MySpace to My Place*, with *The Men's Guide to Snagging Women Online*. In that book, I introduced myself as a former shy kid who developed a knack for meeting women, first from local phone chatlines ("party lines") and eventually chatrooms once AOL became insanely popular in the 90's. The fundamentals learned in those interactions have morphed into email, instant messenger and now social networking sites.

In *The Men's Guide to Snagging Women Online*, I broke down the game that helped me succeed in bringing many women off the internet to "real life". The game was so good, that many women bought that book and urged me to do a follow up—just for the ladies. Almost a year later, I released my second book, "*From MySpace to My Place: The Ladies' Guide to Finding Mr. Right or Mr. Right Now Online*", specifically targeting the needs and concerns of the female audience. But you *knew* that wasn't all! The world of social networking sites is just too big!

Why ANOTHER social networking dating book?

Don't get me wrong—my first two books are **heavy** on game. In fact, if you do not have both of them, please visit http://www.MySpaceToMyPlace.com, Amazon.com or your local Barnes and Noble Bookstore to get your copy. (If it's not on the shelf, approach the cute lady in the green apron and ask her to order it for you…then exchange numbers!)

Although I dropped some "pimp-tight" game in each of those titles, Facebook is a social networking site unlike any other. What actually makes Facebook *unique* is its *uniformity*. While sites like MySpace allow you to import music, wallpaper, and facilitate creative HTML coding, Facebook makes it particularly challenging to distinguish yourself and establish your own identity. You cannot change your background, change font colors and sizes, nor add profile music—at least without the use of applications. Simply put, Facebook makes it more of a challenge to be unique. And as a guy, establishing your uniqueness to Facebook chicks isn't just important—it's *vital*. But don't worry…I got you covered! Proceed.

In addition, Facebook contains other elements that have been (up until recently) absent from MySpace, such as *tagging*, along with *poking* others, sending gifts, popular applications (i.e. "Honesty Box"), and displaying intimate details of your relationship status. Arguably, the most popular feature of Facebook is the "News Feed" which can alert all of your online friends to your every move. The vibe of Facebook is also different. While MySpace has more of a "fun" and "light" feeling to many of its users, Facebook is normally seen as MySpace's "upscale" counterpart. In the world of "social networking", Facebook is a bit heavier on the networking aspect. Fellas, do not fret. I am going to show you how to "milk" the hell out of these features and the vibe of Facebook.

WHAT'S THE POINT OF ALL THIS?

Let me be serious with you for a second. Growing up, I didn't have an ounce of style, "swagger" or game. I was deathly afraid of women and made countless mistakes. I'm no different than most guys. Yet, I was blessed with the opportunity to grow up in different states and meet all types of people who gave me an insight into many aspects of life, *including* game. I've grown up with it, studied it, and live with it. This book isn't about magic tricks. These aren't deceptive techniques. It's not a "pick up" guide. It's *better*. I'm totally convinced that the lessons and skills you will acquire in this book will not only make you a better online mack—but also a more confident guy. If you are single and purchased this guide to enhance your dating life, I want to stress the subject of safe sex. Always wrap it up. Only *you* can prevent fires—down there. And as I write this book today, I continue to meet women online. I *live* this. And if you have questions, I will answer them as best I can at www.facebookdatebook.com.

For the dozens of you who've written me for tailored Facebook advice, this is for you! And if you happen to be a lady with this book, be prepared for some *serious* game! You are in for a treat as well. Take off your shoes, grab a comfy seat and peep game!

Chapter One – Your Profile

Welcome back to your Facebook profile, fellas. I'm assuming you have Facebook—if you don't have it by now, *where have you been?* Unless you just started using computers yesterday, there's no excuse for not having an account. Let me express again that I do not work for Facebook, nor do I have any affiliation with the company. Yet, this website is an important vehicle for networking *AND* meeting women. I know by experience which I will get to later! If by chance you are the .5% of the population without a profile, log onto www.facebook.com right now and sign up!

Here are the things to keep in mind when creating your profile:

1. Establish your identity
2. Appear with cute women
3. Shut up!
4. Manage your relationship status properly
5. Tailor your "Looking For" section appropriately
6. Separate yourself from the pack

Establish your Identity

Similar to my first book, *The Men's Guide to Snagging Women Online* I will first tell you that it is best to first assess who you are. This means being true to yourself. If you're a big dude who loves to eat meat, don't try to pass yourself off as a vegetarian. If you don't like sports, do not pretend to be a Redskins fan. Not only are you being deceitful to those who you will come across, but you are lying to *yourself.* And although it may not seem like it, guys who hold themselves in the highest esteem are the ones who get the most (and best) women. If you want others to respect you, you must first respect yourself. As they say, "to thyself always be true." Remember that.

However, let's be real…you still want to accentuate the best parts of your persona and downplay your shortcomings. While you may be proud of your double-jointed finger or your ability to turn your eye-lids inside out, you might want to keep that under wraps on your profile page. Instead, don't be afraid to highlight some achievements and things that separate you from the pack.

How do you express your uniqueness? Here are some important tips:

1. **Pick a creative nickname.** As I will get into later, I had an encounter with Supermodel and Television Host, Tyra Banks who referred to me as "Rico Suave" on national tv. Therefore I took on that name on my Facebook profile and recount the experience to women who ask me about my selection. Whatever it is, make sure there's a story behind it. Plus it contributes to your *swag* or style. Be forewarned that Facebook *may* get anal about choosing a nickname, so be careful. I suggest making your "middle name" your nickname, while keeping the rest of your name authentic.

2. **Create attention-getting status messages.** A status message is simply a short update, letting people know what you're doing or saying, similar to what is used on Twitter. This is a major tool in your arsenal for getting women to notice you. There is no limit to how creative status messages can get and fellas…this is your bait. Inciting responses through your status message can make you a superstar—whether it's quotes, simple statements or controversial topics. ***Plus it will allow women to properly choose you.*** More on this in chapter 6.

3. **Pick a fly main photo.** I'll get to that later in the chapter.

Appear with cute women

Fellas, I cannot express how important this is. There is nothing that gets a woman's attention more than another woman—the finer, the better. You see, women are naturally competitive amongst themselves. Let me dive into this a bit.

Have you ever walked by the ladies room at a nightclub and seen how all of the women are fixing and preening themselves in the mirror? Do you notice how seriously they put themselves together? While some of this is to garner attention from you guys, it is *more* about making *her* stand out against her competition. This is why it often seems like it is easier to get a girlfriend once you already have one. Having a chick on your arm makes you seem unattainable and therefore a challenge. It elevates your image and drives females to compete over you. This female-to-female competition gives you a distinct social and potentially sexual advantage over women.[1]

Here's the key—be subtle! For every three to five pictures, have *one* with another woman or multiple women. You don't want to overdo it or it'll give you the appearance of trying too hard. Also, make sure she is cute—even if it means you have to get your buddy to snap a photo of you and a girl you just met at a lounge or the club. If you only have one or two female friends, that's okay! One fly female is better than ten turkey vultures!

Shut up!

Seriously, fellas. The single, most common mistake guys make on their social networking profiles is the fact that they put up

---

[1] Unger, Rhonda K. "Women, psychology and evolution." Handbook of the Psychology of Women and Gender. Page: 57. Year Published: 2001.

their entire life story. Nobody really needs to know all of your school club affiliations, dating back to seventh grade. Facebook makes this no easier! It's easy on Facebook to go overboard as they ask you everything from your activities and occupation to your favorite quotes—they might as well ask for your social security number!

Fellas trust me on this one…leave some of these fields blank (they will not appear on your profile and things will still look normal). At the very least, keep these sections brief. As I say all the time, a mysterious man is alluring to women, as it allows them to project their fantasies and desires upon the unknown—which is *you*. Keep it cool and preoccupy her with the task of "prying" you open, which we will get into later! Then you can work on prying *her* open later!

Relationship Status

I'm assuming you are single or at least in an open relationship. If you are in a committed relationship, I do not condone cheating and wave all responsibility should you use the game in this book to cheat! I don't want any angry letters from your girl if she finds my book on your coffee table! (At least hide it underneath your mattress).

I do not see any problem indicating your relationship status on Facebook—it is simply a matter of preference. I've personally chosen to omit my status due to a bad experience. During a recent relationship, my ex-girlfriend would run to Facebook in the heat of an argument and change our relationship status. Many times I wouldn't know until hours or even a day or two later when I logged in and saw messages from friends, telling me that they were sorry about my "break up". Not long after the relationship, I had the opportunity to go on the *Tyra Banks Show*® and explain how it all went down. To see that clip, go to: http://www.youtube.com/FlynessPublishing.

"Looking For?" Section

On Facebook there is a "Looking For" section where you can indicate what you're on Facebook for: 1) Friendship, 2) Dating, 3) A Relationship, and 4) Networking.

Maybe I'm reading into this a little more deeply…but screw it. FELLAS, I do not care if you're the loneliest dude on Earth— do *not* check the boxes that say you're looking for "Dating" or "A Relationship". When females see this, it sends them a message that you're desperate. After all, who wants a *needy* guy? No woman wants a leech. While it is generally cool for women to indicate what they want, you must give the aura that you don't *need* a relationship. As chauvinist as it might sound, *always* give the impression that these females need *you*. Capische?

Separate yourself from the pack

Unless you were blessed enough to look like Brad Pitt or R&B singer "Ginuwine", you're going to have to put in a little work to discover and exploit your niche. So ask yourself what makes you fly? How do you stand out? Think back to the times women have given you compliments—what was it on?

Using myself as an example, women have always complimented me on my arms, as well as my knowledge of many other languages and cultures. Therefore, I make it a point to show off my strong suits. You do the same. For instance, one of my Facebook friends has a *serious* hair style. His hair is extra *crispy* or neat. From time to time, he'll post his main pic with just a shot of his hair cut and the ladies notice. Don't go overboard, but be original.

PHOTOS

Of all the social networking sites in existence, Facebook is the only site to date where I have regularly seen folks with literally hundreds and even thousands of photos. Although MySpace is catching up in terms of the technology, Facebook makes uploading and arranging multiple photos very easy. Good thing? Not necessarily. Here's why uploading too many photos may bite you in the ass.

About six months ago, I got an email from a female on Facebook who asked me to critique her photos. She told me that while she was good-looking, educated, and had great conversational skills, it seemed like the only dudes she could meet—especially online—were losers and guys with no ambition. She said that she just couldn't understand it and thought she'd ask for advice since she's heard of my books. So you know I had to pull out my magnifying glass and get my "Sherlock Holmes" on.

Her page, at first glance seemed decent. As a matter of fact, this girl was cute. Not a dime—but cute. In her main picture, it looked like she was at a formal dinner. Her hair was neat, her makeup was done and overall she seemed presentable…that is, until I clicked on the link, "View Photos of…" I immediately did a double take at a photo that showed this woman at a club "backin' it up" on a guy. It was not a flattering photo. Beyond the fact that her hair looked horrible, there was a big sweat stain underneath this girl's armpit. My stomach churns just thinking about that picture. The worst part about her profile, was that there were many more unflattering photos of her, which were likely the root cause of her problem.

I went ahead and told the girl that she might want to cut down on her photos as many of them didn't flatter her. Her excuse was that her friends kept "tagging" her without her knowledge. ("Tagging" is a way for others to publicly identify you in a photo—I will get into this more later as it can be a GOOD thing as well). She admitted that she liked having hundreds of photos of herself and didn't think anything was wrong with it.

The moral of this story is that it's better to have 20 out of 20 good photos rather than 500 out of 1000 good photos. Personally I keep my photos to a minimum and find myself deleting more than adding. Yet, it is a matter of preference— just make sure they are flattering. Women *will* disqualify you if she spots anything in a photo that sets off a "red flag" in her head. Make sure that you are looking fly and presentable in every shot.

Here are some tips which will improve your "photo game":

1. Invest in a high quality digital camera so that your photos will be crisp, clear and sharp.

2. Make sure your clothes fit properly and are ironed.

3. Make sure the background of your photo is NEAT.

4. Avoid bathroom photos (this is getting old).

5. Make sure that you have some photos with attractive women (I mentioned this in *The Men's Guide* as well).

6. Keep your clothes ON…getting butt-naked makes you look desperate for attention.

7. Have photos taken in different settings—the restaurant, on vacation, the beach, at a wedding, etc.

8. Smile from time to time.

Do not resort to taking shirtless photos! It makes you look desperate!

Overall fellas, exude confidence and style at all times, never appear needy and have fun with it. If you do it right, you are bound to receive some "pokes". Now that your profiles are in order, it's time to find some Facebook females.

Chapter Two – Finding and Landing Prospects

C hapter two in *The Men's Guide* already does an excellent job with breaking down the *types* of women there are and how to identify them online. I will expand on this in Chapter 3, in "The Breakdown".

As opposed to MySpace, even the *way* in which you find females on Facebook is a tad different. First off, make sure you belong to a large regional network that is not far from where you live. If you live in a small town, make sure that you put your nearest major city in your network. (This feature can be accessed by going to "Account Settings" then by clicking on the "Networks" tab). Belonging to a large network will increase your visibility among attractive women in your vicinity.

While it is possible to *find* people by clicking on your network, similar to MySpace's *browse* feature, Facebook is more conducive to "schmoozing" your way into her world.

Below are the best ways to find women on Facebook:
1. Friend or relative of a friend
2. Someone you currently or used to go to school with
3. Someone you **used to** work with (I do not recommend getting at females you **currently** work with)
4. Someone you met at a business function
5. Someone on a mutual Facebook invite list or Facebook group

Friend of a Friend (FOAF)

Point blank—getting at a Friend of a Friend or "FOAF", is the easiest and perhaps the most common way to bag chicks on Facebook. I'd like to personally thank the Facebook developers for the "friends you have in common" feature which gives you the fuel to start conversations with females.

One of the smoothest ways to score a "FOAF" is by finding pictures which include her and your common friend. The photo will give you all the info you need to message the FOAF with little to no effort! They key is, find something *in* the photo and make a comment about it. Just like in real life, nothing should be "coined". There is no such thing as a "good pickup line"—whether on or offline. Just use the situation around you and vibe. The possibilities here are endless. Example…

Say you see a photo of your common friend (let's call her Ashley) and the FOAF (let's call her Tiffany) at a party and your friend, Ashley, is acting extra silly, clumsy or stupid. You could then message Tiffany something like,

> "I felt sorry for you at that party with my friend Ashley. When she acts that way, I usually put her on timeout ;)"

(Including the wink is very important to ensure that she isn't taking you too seriously). Is it that easy? Pretty much. This is the thing fellas—as long as you are *smooth* like this, she will respond positively, if she's interested. And chances are, if you've followed chapter one's guidelines, you will have a high rate of success. And if you need some "technical support" contact me directly at http://www.facebookdatebook.com. Moving on…

A past or present schoolmate

Finding a past or present schoolmate on Facebook is easy as well. Provided you have already listed your school in your

"Education and Work" section, you can browse for your prospects by going to the "Find Friends" section of the website. A major drawback is that many of the women have profiles which are not viewable until you become Facebook Friends—or at least until she sends you a message. In this instance, it makes it easier if you two share at least one mutual friend. If you do, it will be listed when you attempt to view her profile.

Someone you USED to work with

I'll say this a thousand times and I'll say it again—it is generally a BAD idea to become romantically involved with someone that you currently work with. This can be career suicide, especially in a shaky job market. Facebook does not help either; many employers have their own networks online and it is quite possible for an employee to find you, especially if you go by your full name. For that matter, I'd stray away from incorporating *anyone* from your job with your Facebook page. Given that Facebook is more social than professional, it is easy to get carried away with your status updates. In fact, some Facebook users have been fired as a direct result of what they put on their Facebook profiles. Not long ago, CNN did a feature story on a teenager was fired for writing, "I'm bored at work" in her Facebook status.[2] There have been many more stories similar to this one. Who wants to watch what they say so closely?

So fellas, I don't care how cute she is. I don't care how much she may like you. If a fling or a relationship does not work out, imagine how awkward that may prove for your working environment. What if she becomes your superior?

Fellas, fight the urge. If you cannot afford to lose your job, do

[2] Lo, P.K. "Fired Over Facebook Status." NBC San Diego. March 3, 2009.
http://www.nbcsandiego.com/around-town/archive/Fired-Over-Facebook-Status.html

not get with a co-worker. Facebook has tens of millions of users—you can skip her.

A business relationship

Unlike someone who works for your employer who you may see on a regular basis, someone you meet at a conference or networking gala is fair game—as long as dealing with her does not jeopardize your career. On more than one occasion, I've met females at conferences, rallies, voter registration drives, etc. exchanged a few pleasantries and offered my business card. Though I prefer to exchange numbers and move it directly to the phone, a business environment makes this more of a challenge. It's especially hard if you are around other people. In most cases you can't go from a group discussion on economics to sliding a female your number. Not mackish. Instead, exchange business cards and playfully get her Facebook information. And if she has Facebook, that will be an easy way to transition to the phone and to a date. I've done it, it works, and I'll be damned if I'm not doing it as you're reading this!

A mutual Facebook group or Invite List

Simple. Pick any Facebook group or event guest list that you are a part of and browse the others in that group or event list. This is great because you already know that you two share a common interest. The rest is a no brainer. Simply send a "courtesy message" making a comment or asking a question about the group/event. Here's an example:

> "Hey I saw you were also on the Sky Bar Event list. I've never been before…any idea if it's going to be good?"

MECHANICS OF YOUR FIRST MESSAGE

Gone are the days where you are sending every female the SAME message, hoping that one will "bite". (If you're doing that, it's time to drop the habit). As I explained in *The Men's Guide*, I used to do this constantly and enjoyed some success. Yet it disables your ability to think on your feet and does nothing to sharpen your "playa skills". Females are smarter than you may think and can usually tell when your messages aren't personal.

So what's a good first message on Facebook? I've gotten this question *many* times in my Facebook inbox and the answer is, "it depends." What does she have on her page? Who are her friends? What does she enjoy doing? What are her photos like? When you think about it, it's easy to look at someone's profile and use the "intel" you find to ask a question or make a comment that will draw out a reply.

To start, don't place too much emphasis on coming up with a catchy subject. Unlike MySpace, Facebook allows its users to read the first line of a message without opening it. A simple "Hi" or "Interesting page" will suffice for a subject.

Focus your energy on writing a short, but sweet first message. Since Facebook is more personal than MySpace and many other social networking sites, consider telling her how you found her page. It's as simple as saying, "Saw you on my friend Jasmine's wall" or "Wow, you know Josh?" That will put her mind at ease in the event she takes you as a stalker. Follow up with two or three more sentences, **maximum.** With what? I'm glad you asked. Keep reading.

If her page is private, you can still make a comment or ask a question about something in her photo. Whatever the case, make it relevant to something about *her*. Yet, **do not** fall into the trap of complimenting her on her *physicals* or her beauty. Leave that for the other online suckers. Many women I know have shown me how inundated their inboxes are of messages complimenting them. If you go to my YouTube page (http://www.youtube.com/FlynessPublishing), I have a video with a promo model who goes through some of the crazy messages she gets. Messages like, "You are so fine" and worse, "You made my dick hard" are **not** going to help you.

Again, women are attracted to men who show themselves to be at least their equivalent. Make sure that your messages give her room to expand on an answer. "How" and "why" questions almost always force the answering person to give more than a one-word answer, if she's interested. Examine her answer to gauge her interest.

Be mindful that the following examples should only be used when applicable:

Ambiguous compliments

"Your photography skills aren't bad…didn't really expect that when I came to your page. How did you learn?"

"Most of the females I've met in [your city] were sorta raggedy. You seem cool though…how did that happen? :) " (Adding the smiley is *key* here, as it prevents her from taking you too seriously).

Seeking Advice

"You seem like you know a lot about Houston…where can I get some good Mexican food?"

"You read [title of a book on her page]? How was it?"

Be especially careful with your ambiguous compliments as you have a greater chance of offending the girl if you're not careful. When in doubt, add a smiley :) or a wink ;) if the message could be misinterpreted. I have many more examples of ambiguous compliments in the "Inflate-Deflate" section of *The Men's Guide*. If you need some further assistance tailoring a message to a lady, go to http://www.facebookdatebook.com and contact me for assistance.

READING HER REPLY

Okay, I'm assuming you found a cutie and sent her a message, right? Good. Now that you've sent your message, what happens? Well the first thing you must realize is if she doesn't message you back, she is either uninterested or hasn't logged in since you sent the message. And if you happen to notice she's made another update to her page, such as changing her photo or status since you sent her the message, **she is NOT interested** or at least **not interested enough**. Either way, move on! Next! Fellas, do not kid yourselves and write a woman multiple times if she hasn't written back. By the time you send your second or third note, not only is she spreading the word that you're a stalker, but you are subconsciously telling yourself that you need to "sweat" and hound females. It takes a lot of strength to move on…but it's necessary. Hold onto your pride and mack on, playa!

However, if she replies, that doesn't necessarily mean she's genuinely interested, either. If she does reply, try to put yourself in her shoes.

If she's interested or at least open to getting to know you, she will respond positively and will likely leave you an opening to continue the conversation, such as asking you a question in return. Other women will go on and on in a reply, which is a good thing. A woman who talks you ear off may seem annoying, but the more she talks, the more comfortable she is in expressing herself to you. And in my book, comfort = panties. ☺

However, if her reply is brief and neutral, it's best that you move on. Don't even reply. Again, you cannot "win" her interest. At this point, you either have it or you don't.

Here is an example of a good first message, based on what we've gone through so far:

> *Oh, I see you know Ashley…interesting. Most of the females I've met in Brooklyn were sorta raggedy. You actually seem cool though…how did that happen? :)*

IF SHE MAKES THE FIRST MOVE

When you receive a message, a friend request, or even a "poke" from a lady on Facebook, it is no accident. This lady is showing interest. Something about your picture or profile caught her attention. If you are interested, continue the conversation as discussed earlier in the chapter. Keeping in mind how sensitive women are, you may want to tone down or maybe even completely eliminate giving her an ambiguous compliment in the first message. By making the first move, you have a significant advantage, as she has likely veered out of her comfort zone to get your attention. Proceed! If by chance you are not interested in a woman who "makes a move", it is okay to deny the friend request or hide the poke. If she messages you, it is most polite to politely thank her without continuing the conversation. (If you have trouble with a woman who's relentless in her pursuit, I will get into that in Chapter 10).

Chapter Three – The Breakdown

B efore we get into this chapter, grab a comfy seat. **This is a long one!** (It's called "The Breakdown" for a reason!) I cannot over-emphasize the importance of having standards. Too many guys in this day and age are happy (or at least content) with having *any* woman, especially if it's a booty call. This is especially true for guys under 21 who are generally very inexperienced. Many guys, especially young men, are not used to being more selective and scrupulous about their dating choices. After all if you are more selective, won't that drain your supply of ladies? **Not especially.** In fact, you'd be surprised at how many women will upgrade themselves to your liking. Many women find a blunt, yet confident man attractive.

Fellas, do not settle for "whackness" whether it's a one-night stand or a full-blown commitment. Many women test guys at the beginning of relationships to see what they can get away with. Always use this opportunity to pass her test by being a real man. The same goes for online. Man up!

Say you see a cute woman online: a pretty face, nice butt, good size rack, but…she has a disrespectful attitude? NOPE! What if she insists that you take her out for an expensive dinner on a first date? NOPE! What if she is combative and places demands on you? NOPE!

In this chapter, I will be dividing women into three main categories: **1.) "NOPE"**—the women you stay far away from; **2.) "SLOPE"**—the women who present an "uphill" issue that you may or may not want to pursue, and **3.) "POKE"**—the women you want! (Keep in mind that I do **not** actually recommend actually using the "poke" feature until you've come to know her on some level. More on that in Chapter 5.

THE NOPE CATEGORY: Women to avoid at all costs

Starvin' Carmens

I cannot remember a time when there were as many "hungry" females, as there are today. Not to knock all women, but far too many females insist on being "wined and dined" from day one. A starvin' Carmen can be any woman who insists that you spend a significant amount of money on her too soon. Fellas, **never** spend a large amount of money on a first date. At this stage you don't know her from a hole in the wall. Plus, what incentive does she have to get to know you if you've already volunteered yourself as her sugar daddy? In many cases, starvin' Carmens already have boyfriends or even husbands and just want you around to boost her ego and fill her stomach. If you have to pay to date a woman, you might as well cut to the chase and get a prostitute. Forget that! Leave these women alone.

So how do you know if you are staring at the profile of a hungry female? The primary way to identify her is if she hints at you taking her out to eat. Don't worry fellas, these women will let you know relatively soon. If it doesn't happen during the conversation flow online, it will come up on the phone. If it does, say something like, "No, I don't know you like that. You have to earn it." (Make sure you do this with a smirk, so you don't appear militant). If she accepts your counter offer, she's still in the game. If she balks, excuse yourself and send her hungry ass a supermarket coupon. (Yeah, I said it).

Hood Chicks/Trailer Trash

I shouldn't even need this section. However, there are too many guys who do not mind and actually seek out trash and "thugettes". Fortunately Facebook is not known for attracting too many of these. Yet, you still want to be careful. Not only does this type of female attract problems, but keep in mind that behind every one of these "thugettes", is a thug dude lurking around somewhere. Is getting ass really worth getting stabbed?

Here are some signs that she's probably done time:

1. Her photos show her with multiple tattoos depicting guns or weapons.
2. She won't smile in any of her photos.
3. She is throwing up gang signs in her photos.
4. All of her friends look like they belong in a police line up—even the girls.
5. Every time she updates her status, it's another RIP (sad, but true).

Disrespectful Women

As you can probably tell by now, I am *very* big on mutual respect, as you should be too. This is extremely important. Simply put, never tolerate disrespect from a woman (or anyone for that matter). It is particularly important to maintain respect in your interactions with the ladies. In general, women tend to be more emotional than men, as the wiring in their brains are literally different, thanks to biology and evolution.[3] Combine this with disrespect and this can cost you your well being—even your life in rare cases! (Relax, this is true with only *some* ladies, not all!) Nonetheless, in many instances, it's difficult to tell how potentially disrespectful a woman is until you start messaging each other. As I already touched on, you must respect yourself first, as it is contagious. If you command respect, others will give you respect.

---

[3] Lloyd, Robin. "Emotional Wiring Different in Men and Women." LiveScience. April 2006. http://www.livescience.com/health/060419_brain_wiring.html.

Some excusable, subtle forms of disrespect include her ignoring a question you asked or her insisting that you call her, when you've already suggested that she calls you. However, this is more of a *test* than disrespect. Always pass her tests by manning up! More on that in Chapter 4.

Here are some signs you're dealing with a truly disrespectful woman on Facebook:

1. She pokes fun at you a little too much.
2. She adds any one of your friends and tries to flirt with them.
3. She blatantly ignores any one of your questions.
4. She curses at you for no real reason.
5. Her photos depict her acting out in lewd or offensive ways, e.g. sticking up the middle finger or breaking the law.

Stalkers

A no brainer, right? Duh. No one wants a stalker. But somehow, many of us end up with them, simply because we ignore the signs. We might be blinded by the beauty (or booty). Perhaps we get lonely. Whatever. As a mack and a man, always be careful and pay attention.

This is especially true on Facebook. This social networking site is a stalkers paradise. In most instances stalkers are your lonely or super-clingy women. Therefore these types of women will easily find refuge and relief from being online.

Here are some signs she's probably watching you right now:

1. She's *always* online (watch out for the "Online Now" notification on her chat window).

2. She always comments on your status updates or on your wall.

3. She messages you regardless of whether you reply to her. And will message you *again* to see if you got her previous messages.

So let's say you already have an online stalker or a female you're trying to get rid of. What do you do? That's in Chapter 10!

Crazy Women

Like stalkers and clingy women, this is another type of female you must recognize and cut off before you get her on the phone, let alone a date! In *The Men's Guide* I gave an example of a crazy, young female I dated, named "Daisy." (This is not her real name—just a nickname given to protect her identity). I was blinded by her beauty. Although we weren't exclusively involved, I allowed her fly and sexy appearance to cloud my judgment. I dated her *way* too long and ignored the warning signs that I was dealing with a psycho. Literally. After only days of *kickin it*, she began leaving me freaky voicemail messages, told me that she loved me, and would call me at least five times a day. You might think she'd be a stalker right? Wrong. Her cousin revealed to me that "Daisy" was an ex-mental patient and had actually attempted to slit her wrists. A few weeks into meeting "Daisy" online, she actually attempted to slit her wrists because I was unable to see her at her request. That's when I had to cut her off, no pun intended! To my knowledge she is still alive and well, so no worries! My lesson here? Look out for the loonies! As soon as you spot a crazy woman on Facebook, do not give her a second look.

Here are the signs your "Daisy" may be crazy:

1. She seems to be obsessed with one thing and it's all over her profile.

2. Her message responses seem to be a little "off".

3. She has a fictional figures or cartoon photos in her photo galleries (be careful—this might be a sign that she's underage too).

4. Her friends exhibit any one of the above symptoms.

5. Her profile page makes absolutely no sense.

Co-workers

No! As stated in the previous chapter, getting romantically involved on *any* level with someone from work is a bad idea, especially if it's a job you *need*. Part of being a man is being stable. And fellas, stability is *not* potentially mixing business with pleasure! No warning signs necessary! If she's in your "working network" on Facebook, do not get at her. Keeping the boundaries in mind, it *is* okay to friend request her and get at her friends.

Multiple Baby Daddy Women

This is not to criticize women who have more than one child from different fathers. There are a couple of women I know in this category, one of whom is a dear friend. However, the term "multiple baby daddy" refers to women who have children with men outside of the confines of a marriage and even without being in a relationship. In extreme cases, these are the women seen on the Jerry Springer and Maury Povich Shows trying to figure out who are the fathers of their babies. The more "baby-daddies" she has, the worse.

A woman who was a young mother in this situation can be excused to an extent as maturity sets in over time. It is also understandable if she has a child or two, depending on her circumstances. But if she's still getting knocked up by different guys in her mid to late 20's, it's time to hit "block user" before it even gets to the message exchange! As Facebook grows in population, so do the population of these females. Beware. You don't want to be baby daddy number five. Imagine the drama.

Here are some signs she is ready to have *your* baby:

1. You already see a bunch of children in her photo galleries, although she is *not* a teacher.

2. She exhibits any of the hood chick or trailer trash characteristics.

3. She's obsessed with cartoons and has pictures of them in her photo galleries.

4. Early in a message exchange, she mentions that you would have cute kids together.

5. She lets you know that she hates protection and rarely uses it (I've had this happen)!

Long distance women

As discussed in Chapter 2, you should aim to find women in your network, or at least in your vicinity. As cute as she might be, it makes absolutely **no** sense to kick game to a woman if you live in Maryland and she lives in California. It is simply not realistic to think that anything will come out of an "online thang" with a chick from the other side of the country. Even if you have the means and the energy to do so, why bother? In some cities, not having a car can really limit your options. Make sure that you have a plan for how and where you two will meet. Be practical and realistic.

However, there are *three* exceptions to long distance women. First off, you can use these women to get at other women, such as her friends. Keep it 100% platonic and treat her like a "homie." Then when you spot one of her cute friends in your area, use the FOAF technique described in Chapter 2 to get to know the friend. The second exception to getting at long distance women is when you use her for "groundwork in a wall war", where she will boost your reputation through public flirting. (More on that in Chapter 6). The last exception is if you two will cross paths while one of you is on vacation. If that's the case, you want to continue with the conversation flow around a week before you two are in the same area—therefore the intrigue is not lost. After the message exchange, have her call you at a specific time and set up a time to hang out. I've done this many times—yet you must remember, timing is everything.

Underage Women

Once again, I should not have to tell you guys. But please, leave the young girls alone! There are simply too many women of legal age to deal with on Facebook. If you have a thing for "high school seniors" at least find out when her birthday is and wait until she reaches that magic number. I'm not going to take the stand if you decide to meet "Dora The Explorer's" number one fan off Facebook. If in doubt of what is legal in your state (or country), go to Google.com and type in "Age of Consent Laws" and look for your country.

Here are some signs she's under age:

1. sH3 sP3LLS hER w0RD5 LYk3 th15 – sEe?
2. She refers to her friends as her "bff's" (Best Friend Forever).
3. Her page seems too girly, i.e. hearts and roses all over the place.
4. All her friends are young.
5. Her interests include anything by The Jonas Brothers, Bow Wow or Soulja Boy.

Con-Artists

Fortunately, Facebook has done a pretty good job at dissuading the con-artists from taking over the site, similar to the way they devoured MySpace. Nevertheless, be cautious of "female" con-artists. The number one sign you are being set up for a scam is receiving a friend request from an unusually attractive woman from a different network or even a different country. After accepting the request, she will try to guide the dialog to the instant messenger, rather quickly. After about five minutes of chatting she will do either one of two things: 1) Ask you to go to her webcam link or adult site, or 2) send your name and address to her.

Here are the signs she's a crook:

1. She only has guy friends (normally from different countries) and will only have one or two photos.
2. Her grammar is bad.
3. Her messages seemed crafted and long.
4. She shows too much interest too soon.
5. She has links on her page, asking to click to see her "other" profile page.
6. Her profile picture is either too blurry or too "perfect"-looking (it was probably stolen).

Scandalous Women

A scandalous woman is perhaps the worst type of woman to deal with. Similar to hood and trailer trash women, this is another type of female that can affect your well-being and even your life. On more than one occasion I have met women online who I came to find out later were already involved or even married! A friend of mine was actually invited into a females home for some "action", while her boyfriend was at work. He participated, but felt bad after seeing photos of the two together, in an apparent "happy" relationship. Other scandalous women will not hesitate to go after her girlfriends boyfriends. These are the spoiled, drama queens that are impossible to satisfy.

For obvious reasons, this is *not* the business! What if the boyfriend or husband catches you with his woman? And if she's scandalous enough to cheat on her husband with you, what else is she capable of? What if she sets you up to be killed? Fellas, be extremely careful, both on and offline.

Here are some ways to tell if she's nothing but a "skeeze":

1. She's listed as "In a Relationship" or "Married" but she pokes you or sends you a flirtatious message.
2. Her photo galleries consist of her making out with different men.
3. As soon as you two become "Facebook Friends", she friend requests all of *your* male friends.

SLOPE Women: Exercise extreme caution

Women with a "little extra"

Granted, some of you guys like your girls on the "chunky" side. And that's cool if that's what you like. A good number of you however, settle for big girls because that's all you feel you can get. Now *that* is a bad move. Always remember that it is better to be alone and uphold your standards, rather than settling for a sub par woman…on *any* level.

The reason why I place big girls in the SLOPE Group goes back to why a woman might be overweight in the first place. On one hand, a woman may be predisposed to her weight due to her family genes. Yet, there have been quite a few studies conducted which investigated how trauma and stress often leads to binge eating and weight gain as a result. There has also been some research conducted suggesting that stress itself produces hormones which promote weight gain.[4] Whatever the case, it would then make sense that you'd want to tread lightly around a female who might be dealing with psychological issues. And as a mack who's on top of his game (as you will be after you finish reading this book), you want a lady on top of *her* game too, right? I'm not saying stay away. I'm just urging you to exercise caution.

Assuming you do not prefer your girls large, be mindful that there is a growing trend of ladies who post deceptive photos of themselves online. The "largest" deceptive group is the big women.

Here are some ways to tell if she's hiding that "baby fat":

1. All of her photos are from the chest, up.

2. She has very few photos of herself.

3. Most of her photos are of her as a younger child.

4. She puckers her lips or takes pictures with a "fish face".

5. In her "interests" section she makes multiple references to food or cooking.

6. She leans over or even sticks out her butt to distract from the rest of her body.

7. She only has pictures of certain body parts up close— usually the lips, breasts or butt.[5]

---

[4] Stöppler, Dr. Melissa Conrad. William C. Shiel Jr., MD. "Stress, Hormones, and Weight Gain." Medicine.net. Feb 2007. http://www.medicinenet.com/script/main/art.asp?articlekey=53304.

[5] Nasheed, Tariq. "MySpace Deception." Mack Lessons Radio Show. 2007. http://www.macklessonsradio.com/index/page/3.

8. All of her girlfriends are big.

9. Her hair is always down to cover up her cheeks and neck.

10. She adjusts the properties of her photos to make everything appear thinner, including her.

Young women (Ages 18-21)

This one depends on a number of factors. It depends on what you're looking for, as well as your age. This is because women between the ages of 18 and 21 are not usually ready to "settle down". While many of these girls have boyfriends, this is also the demographic that flood the nightclubs every weekend while dancing on each other and doing outlandish things. These are referred to as attention-whores (as I will get to in a minute). Therefore, I recommend leaving these women alone if you are looking for something serious. Also, be ready for more bullshit stemming from immaturity.

On the plus side, these women are usually more carefree, less baggage-laden and in tip-top physical condition. In fact, I kicked it with an extremely attractive 18 year old from MySpace recently who fit everything I described above to the "T"—immature, yet fun and physically fly. Finding her age is easy—just look at her birth date as it is usually displayed at the top of her profile (unless she elects not to show it, which is rare).

Here's how to tell if she's too immature to deal with:

1. She has too much useless garbage on her Facebook page like Facebook gifts, children's applications, surveys and games.

2. sH3 sp3LLs lyK3 thY5 (She spells like this).

3. Most of her photos are group shots with her and her friends (a sign she may be co-dependent on her friends).

Older women (30 and above)

Women above the age of 30 come with their own pros and cons. Once many single women hit the magical age of 30, many are psychologically affected by the pressure society places on them to mate and "procreate". Biologically, her body is becoming less fertile as well. Although some ladies are perfectly okay with being single at 30+ years of age, it drives others up the wall. These women also have a higher chance of having children from previous relationships, which is another issue altogether. As a result, she may develop a jaded outlook on life.

As a side note, I blame many relationship authors for targeting this group with horrific dating advice. Some examples include superficial time limits placed on when to have sex with a man, along with promoting attitudes that sabotage relationships long before they've had a chance to take shape.

All of the above could spell despair for any woman once she hits the age of 30. Thankfully, there are many ladies who have overcome these hurdles, by staying grounded in who she is. In most cases, these are the ladies that are spiritual, still in shape, eat healthy, and foster a non-combative and cool disposition. If you come across a lady over 30 (or of any age), look for these qualities.

Here are some signs that she's an old hen that needs to be "plucked" from your Facebook datebook:

1. She posts note after note about men who've done her dirty (Many times these come in the form of poems).
2. She posts link after link of relationship articles, most of which are critical only of the male gender.

3. You can see a public argument on her wall with another guy.

4. Something on her page says something like "Men are dogs" or "Men ain't shit".

5. She is overweight, has multiple baby's fathers or exhibits multiple signs of the NOPE ladies, described earlier in the chapter.

You do not need to avoid these ladies altogether—again, I've kicked it with many older women who had themselves together. Just remain cognizant of potential pitfalls!

Sexual Freaks

I *know* you probably think this is a typo. After all, how could you possibly place sex-crazed freaks in the SLOPE category? Remember my story about "Crazy Daisy"? Exactly. I'm not necessarily saying to leave the freaky women alone. In fact, if you're a single and mature enough to handle it, do your thing. However, always ask yourself *why* she is the way she is. In some cases, she may have been abused growing up. Perhaps she is psychologically turning to sex to garner attention from guys. Truth be told, be careful of these diseases and always stay cognizant of STD rumors. Better safe than sorry. Moreover, make certain that she's at least truthful. I have countless example (both personal and from friends) of women cheating on their boyfriends and even husbands just to "get their freak on." As I said in *The Men's Guide,* hittin' that ass isn't worth catching one *in* the ass! Fellas, just make sure that "hitting her wall" won't lead to taking a fall!

Here are some signs that she may not be worth the "poke":

1. She exhibits any of the signs of a crazy woman.

2. She will stop at nothing to get it *all* the time, even if it means cheating on her boyfriend to be with you.

3. She suggests, either directly or indirectly that she doesn't want you to wear a condom, which can lead to….

4. She has a bump or lesion situation "down there".

Scantily clad women

You might be thinking I lost my mind on this one too, but you have to use your brain. Again ask yourself *why* things are the way they are. If an attractive woman chooses to disrobe, think about the reasons behind it. This is in the "SLOPE" category because this may be good or it may be bad. Use your intuition and forget your "woodtuition".

On one hand, she might be a "naturalist" who's perfectly fine and content with her body. Or even more so, a freak. However, she could be a woman begging for attention or even a woman who baits in guys just to shut them down for ego gratification. If she's the "bait and switch" type, then she needs to be avoided at all costs. To tell where she fits, proceed in the conversation and watch her replies carefully. If she says anything to try to draw your attention to her pictures, remain cool and sound unphased. Add humor, as we discussed in Chapter 2. Whatever the case, this woman is *only* suited for non-relationship purposes only. In other words, this is a "smash and grab"-type deal. Turning her into "wifey" is like making a kitten bark!

Online Businesswomen

This group includes female authors, website owners, party promoters, and any other female who devotes her page to a business, craft or hustle. Instead of revealing any information on herself, her status updates and notes are usually sales pitches and web commercials. In short, she's using Facebook to put her product(s) on the map. Cool, right? The answer is, "It depends."

Among other girls, I met my ex, an "Online Businesswoman" via my "Honesty Mackin" technique (which I will break down for you in Chapter 8). That situation was cool as she didn't resist too hard when I shifted things away from her product and onto her. That's simply what you do—begin the interaction by taking an interest in what she's doing. Say you come across a cute female who runs a photography studio. You might want to ask what kind of camera she uses or how she got into photography. After an exchange or two, shift the conversation to learning about her. It's all about tact—*ease* into it. Remember, *use her product as bait and get her to a date.*

However, online businesswomen aren't always the best women to "get at." There are instances where they will not pay attention to you, whatsoever, unless you are a potential client or business partner. Once again, business and pleasure do not mix! On more than one occasion, I've met extremely attractive women both on and offline who just wanted *one* thing—business! Whether they realize it or not, many will use their looks to sell their product.

I remember one young woman I met who had her own soft porn site, yet sold a telecommunications service. In her attempt to "pitch" me online, I "macked on" her only to find that she lived with her boyfriend and daughter. Yet it was funny—during our conversation, she tried to convince me that her product was selling because it was good. I never laughed so hard. Her product was outdated, tacky and expensive, yet she tried to convince me that her 30,000 or so online friends were a testament to her product. Turned out she had a half-naked photo set as her default pic, not to mention her photo gallery. In addition she promised to contact persons who were interested in buying into her business. What desperate guy wouldn't go for that?!

Here are some signs she only wants your business and nothing else:

1. She makes it a point to mention her product or service at every possible moment.
2. She has no personal photos or information on her page.
3. She dodges or flat out ignores questions about her personal life.
4. All of her Facebook friends are either clients, desperate guys, or both.
5. She expresses zero interest in you after you reveal a disinterest in her business.

Women with boyfriends

First of all, do not consider getting into anything serious with a lady in a relationship. Even if she leaves her man to be with you, she will likely leave you to be with the next guy! Got it?

So what if you just want some "action?" Fellas, this one depends. Generally you should shy away from a Facebook profile from a lady that lists her as "in a relationship with" or "it's complicated with." While some women do this to keep some guys away, it is usually not worth the hassle in finding out. A major exception could be that she is not from your area and happens to be around for a short period of time. This assures you that your chances of bumping into her man are slim. It's never "player" or cool to fight over another guy's woman. And given the times we are living in, it can be flat out dangerous or even deadly to go down this road. There are plenty of eligible women to choose from!

Attention Whores and Picture Whores

So what exactly *is* an "attention whore?" Simply put, this is a young woman who seeks attention from as many guys as possible. For the most part, younger women go through this phase beginning at around age 17 and can last 3-4 years. In person, she is easily identifiable. And that's the point! She's usually the scantily clad woman rocking the shortest skirt to the party "grinding" on all of her friends. Her biggest thrill is the psychological rush she gets, knowing that guys are staring and gawking at them. These girls literally "get off" on the attention! However, the guys who get with them are usually the thugs or bad boys which show them next to no attention. Yet it is possible to snag an attention whore *without* being a "rough neck." More on that in a second.

Similarly there is the "picture whore." This is simply an attention whore who goes online. This is the girl with the most scandalous, provocative photos imaginable. These include bend-over shots, dancing on stripper poles, and even showing her "goods." She also tends to have the *most* photos on her page. Unlike MySpace, where 100 pictures or more would easily land you in the "picture whore" category, it is relatively easy to accumulate 100 photos between multiple albums on Facebook. It is not uncommon to see upwards of 500 photos in a Facebook profile. Many picture whores easily exceed 1,000 photos.

Handling this type of woman is a two step process. Step one is to show her that you are not like all the other guys who are mystified by her beauty. **Do not** compliment her appearance at all, nor should you make any references to her body. (Don't even tell her she *looks* nice or you risk being lumped in with all the other chumps who've boosted her ego that hour). Step two is to throw her off her "high horse." This is done by giving her an ambiguous compliment as described in the last chapter. As simple as this sounds, you'd be surprised at how many guys fail!

Rather than going off a number, here are some better ways to diagnose a CPW (Certified Picture Whore):

1. She has albums that have no theme—other than just pictures of her.

2. She leaves captions and comments under each of her personal photos, along with responses.

3. She seeks out and takes photos with celebrities (which also classifies her as a groupie).

4. She begs guys to leave her photo comments.

5. She wears tons of makeup and overdresses in all of her Facebook photos—even in her bedroom and bathroom photos.

Bougie Girls

"Bougie" is interpreted by many of those in pop culture as someone who exudes an aura of higher class or even "snobbishness." This comes from the term, "bourgeoisie" which is an old term for someone of a higher, elite class. Depending on who you talk to, "bougie girls" are either stuck up or simply the ones whom are used to the finer things in life. Whatever the case, dealing with these women has its advantages and disadvantages.

On one hand it can be quite rewarding dealing with a bougie girl. These women are typically refined and come from good families. That means money that *you* may have access to if you play it right. In my experiences, these women tend to be a hell of a lot more attractive as well. On the other hand, bougie women all tend to have the same flaws. They tend to be materialistic, self-absorbed, bratty, and in some cases, outright bitches.

If you choose to deal with this girl, always play down her possessions and act as if they don't phase you. Similar to the attention whore, do not act impressed with her *money* or status. Always think and act as if you are the prize.

Here's how to tell when to leave a bougie girl alone:

1. Her profile or status does nothing but play up on her possessions (i.e. "Ooh I just bought the new $2,000 bag!")

2. She constantly updates her status asking people to grade her appearance or style of dress.

3. She never worked a day in her life, yet expects you to have a job.

4. Her profile is devoted to talking about what she *doesn't* like in men.

Virgins

Depending on your expectations of a Facebook encounter, virgins may not be what you want. Though it is rare to encounter a *true* virgin (a woman who has not had *any* sexual contact, whatsoever), there are a few out there. Unless you, yourself are "saving it for marriage", I suggest leaving v-card holders alone. A shining exception is if she's a college freshman.[6] Think about it—meeting people in a brand new environment can lead to a sexual independence. If you meet a virgin in this type of situation, move in quickly. Yet, keep in mind that if you are *really* her "first", there's a great chance she'll develop strong feelings for you. If you do not want a relationship, this is not the best move.

How can you tell if you are dealing with a virgin? It's best to just come out and ask. For this question, wait until the phone call or

---

[6] Flyness, Your Royal. "Recruiting and Sifting Through Prospects." From MySpace To My Place: The Men's Guide to Snagging Women Online. 2008.

first date to find out. Once you start to get "advanced" in your game, you can slip that in a chat.

Religious Women

Similar to virgins, the decision to kick game to a religious female depends on your desires. If you want a church going girl who may look down upon getting physical, then this may be your cup of tea. I personally think it is cool to hang out with a God-fearing woman. Yet, be mindful if she gets "extreme" with it.

Also keep in mind *why* she's religious. Was she raised in the Church? Are her parents religious? Or is she seeking redemption for all the sinning she's done outside the church? If she's religious for the latter reason, there's a high likelihood that you may have a real "super-freak" on your hands. In this case, heed advice from that section.

Here's how to tell if her religion may be getting in the way:
1. Every single status update posted is a scripture lesson.
2. She thinks that kissing on the first date is a sin.
3. The majority of her friends are pastors, bishops, deacons and choir members.
4. She attends church every day of the week.

Celebrities

Impossible, right? Wrong! It is entirely possible to meet celebrities off the internet. As technology has improved over the past couple of years, people who once seemed unattainable are now easily accessible via Facebook. Now how *likely* is it that a superstar will take interest in *you*? This is why a female celebrity belongs in the SLOPE category. In your pursuit of a celebrity, realize that men from the upper echelons of society are trying to court her as well. She is most certainly running into men with money and fame—the prettier she is, the more she'll encounter these men. Any celebrity deals with multitudes of people on a daily basis. A *beautiful* celeb can't get away from gawking, "simpin" men.

However, I've personally met a few television personalities off the internet, most recently a woman who was on a television show. While meeting a celebrity from Facebook might *seem* intriguing, they are people like everyone else.

Bottom line: do you have a chance? Sure. A *good* chance? Probably not. The best think you can do is see which other NOPE, SLOPE, or POKE categories she fits into and mack accordingly. Pay special attention to grabbing her attention in the first note! You never know until you try.

Here's how to tell if you may need to move on from a celeb:

1. Her status updates refer to herself in the third person (a key indicator that someone else is managing her profile).
2. She hasn't replied to your note since her last 1 or 2 logins.
3. She's married or has a boyfriend.
4. She replies to any message from you asking you to buy her album or watch her show on television.
5. She exhibits any one of the warning signs in the NOPE category.

POKE Women: This is your target! Proceed.

Career Women

There is nothing like a career woman. She wakes up in the morning, goes to work, and comes home with a paycheck. In many instances a career woman is financially stable. It's a beautiful thing. Many women with *careers* (as opposed to jobs) have attained at least a Bachelor's degree and earn a decent living. Fellas, these are the ones you want.

Beyond the financial advantages of having someone who is economically self-sufficient, she stands a greater likelihood of being responsible. You cannot party too much in college or you will not graduate. And if you goof off at work—especially in corporate America, you will not last long. The very fact that she has a career should earn her some points. On some level she is responsible and a responsible lady is a necessity.

Intellectual Women

This category almost goes hand in hand with the career women, as it takes brains to make it that far in life. Having an intelligent woman is a *must*, especially when embarking on a potential relationship. No one wants to deal with a mate with the intellect of a rock. To find out her level of intellect, simply look at what she has to say in her Facebook profile, her level of education and the groups she belongs too. And if you should begin to write notes, check her grammar and spelling.

Shy Women

I see opportunity when I come across a shy, yet attractive female. Typically, shy women come from sheltered environments where they rarely had opportunities to express themselves. This is where you come in. Use a Facebook girl's naiveté as an opportunity to show her more about you *and* herself. I've met shy women of all different backgrounds, cultures and ages. Yet they all tend to share one thing in common: their lives have been pretty boring…that is, up until now, fellas. That's where *you* come in.

As I said in *The Men's Guide* many guys let their pride get in the way when getting at shy women. Realize that she may not know how to reply to your first note. Don't necessarily take a "coy reply" as a sign of being dissed. If she's shy, she might need help in the interaction.

Here's how to tell if she's a shy girl *waiting* to be set free:

1. She appears to be overly smart or brainy (check her education level or the books she reads).

2. She lives or used to live in a rural or suburban neighborhood.

3. She shows very subtle hints of interest (a friend request, a poke or any excuse to initiate contact).

4. She dresses ultra conservatively in her photos.

5. Her replies are brief, yet they contain subtle signs of interest (i.e. smiley faces and "lols").

Women who keep to themselves

Nobody wants their business in the streets and I'm sure you don't either. With the advent of the Facebook status feed, a female can publicly embarrass you within *moments* especially if she uses Facebook on her cell phone. This category is important! Always seek a woman who keeps to herself to some extent.

Keeping to yourself to an extent is also a sign of maturity. You might notice that many teenage girls have many best friends or "bffs." At a college party, the female freshmen come in packs. Yet at more "grown and sexy" venues, women over 22 tend to roll with three or less. It is not uncommon to see a woman "rolling dolo" meaning venturing off by herself. Use that to your advantage.

Lastly, a woman who keeps to herself means that her friends have a lesser likelihood of cock-blocking you. Say you arrange to have a date with a woman four days in advance. A younger woman is much more likely to "flake" on you (cancel a date at the last minute) since her friends are a big part of her influence. The more friends she has, the more weak-minded she tends to be.

"Diagnosing" a woman who keeps it to herself is easy. Check her friends list and her wall comments. If you don't see too many people, she likely falls into this category. When unsure, just ask.

Local Women

As explained earlier, a woman that lives within your Facebook network is the way to go. Always make a point to notice what city and even which part of the city she lives in. It should never be inconvenient for you to meet someone off Facebook. And if by chance a woman isn't close by, let the burden be on her to meet up with you. Make sure she's local!

So which lady is best?

At the end of the day guys, a balanced woman is what you want. It is certainly possible to have a quality "bougie" career woman or a good shy, devout Christian woman. No one is perfect and rarely does a female fit entirely in the POKE category.

However, as in any interaction, make sure there is mutual respect and go from there.

Chapter Four – Sealing the Deal

B y this time you should know the mechanics of a first note and you should be ready to move forward with a short dialogue. Yet you *must not* get carried away. Many guys have a tendency to ramble, going on and on in any given note. Just because Facebook allows a lot of room to type your heart away, it does not mean she wants to read your life's story. If you chat too much in a text box, she'll assume you chat too much in person. Women do not find talkative men sexy. As my friend BossMack Topsoil says, "Don't ever let your girl know what you're thinking." At least not at first.

WHAT TO SAY

The most common question I get in my email inbox from men is, "What do I say to women online?" I'll get into some examples in a second. But overall, *always* have the mindset that she has something to gain by associating with you, not vice-versa. In today's society (in the Western world anyway), women are held in a very high regard—particularly their beauty and booty. There is a common mantra in the player community which warns not put "*pussy* on a pedestal." Fellas, you must always converse with women as if *you* are the prize. The minute she feels superior over you is the minute she loses respect for you *and* the minute you lose your chances with her. Don't blow it!

Conversation Flow

Here's how the conversation should flow. Your first message should grab her attention. If it doesn't, leave her alone and move on. But if it does, respond accordingly and always strive to keep her talking about herself. This accomplishes two things: (1) She will feel like she knows you better, and (2) you will remain somewhat of a mystery. Making her feel like she knows you is important when meeting a female on any site, but it is *vital* on Facebook. Moving both quickly *and* carefully are important.

Your next two to four messages should simply flow, based on her responses. And trust me fellas—if she likes you, she will often facilitate good conversation. In the conversation, it's not exactly *what* you say that matters, but *how* you say it. You have four main objectives in conversation flow:

1. Keep her talking.
2. Be interesting and witty.
3. Get her on the phone quickly.
4. Don't screw up.

KEEP HER TALKING

Getting a woman's attention is usually the hardest part. After that, the rest should be a piece of cake. To keep the water flowing, simply remember to ask *how* and *why* questions. Since women are emotional creatures, asking the question, "So how did that make you feel" can usually open the flood gates.

Another tactic is to make comments which incite a response. This will prevent your conversation from sounding like you're interviewing her.

BE INTERESTING

For this section, I strongly recommend getting *The Men's Guide* as there is an entire chapter which shows conversation techniques. But in short, you want to be witty and fun. Lightly tease her about things such as her height (call her a shorty if she's under 5'4), or if she has a perfect-looking smile, ask her if her teeth are real. Find something light to joke about with her. In my opinion, small girls are the easiest to joke around with. For instance, you can joke about never being able to take them to an Amusement Park because she may not meet the height requirement. This shows her you're comfortable in your own skin and are not afraid of being engaging.

Your entire tone should be one of importance. When talking to her, make it seem like *you* are the prize. You want to give the impression that you are totally comfortable with meeting girls. Give her a challenge. Don't be easy—or at least don't make yourself *seem* easy. I'll give an example of a good exchange in a moment.

GET HER TO THE PHONE QUICKLY

It is very important to get her to the phone quickly. Yes, I guess you would technically call *The Facebook Datebook* an online dating book. Guilty. However, your goal is *not* to date her online! You want bring her from Facebook to *your* nook! The way you get her to the phone quickly is to think ahead of the conversation. Before you ask a question to type something, you should already be thinking about how she may react and what you will say.

For instance, your first message may mention her height. In the next message, you could talk about how short girls usually make good cheerleaders, then transition into what she did in school, her life, what she does for fun, etc. Then you can either tell her that she seems cool and suggest a number exchange *or* you can have her call you right then and there. If she's online and is responding to you quickly, move it to the phone. The key here is to not let things drag out. Intrigue is time sensitive! "Yoink" her off Facebook quickly to keep your mysterious aura going!

DON'T SCREW UP

Fellas, use common sense. Don't talk too much. Read or at least glance over her page. Try not to curse too much and definitely do not bring up sex to be on the safe side. Even the "ho-iest ho" will most times act like a Church girl when confronted with sex too soon. Just relax and do not go above the call of duty to try to impress her. That alone will help you stand out from the massive number of punk softies out there.

Other than those four items, go for it! I believe in you.

Here's an example of a conversation:

> *YOU: Most of the females I've met from Brooklyn were sorta raggedy. You actually seem cool though...how did THAT happen? :) By the way, how do you know my friend, Ashley?*

> *LEAH: Ashley's my best friend.....and NO WE ARENT ALL RAGGEDY thankyouverymuch! Lol...thanks for the compliment (I think). How are you?*

> *YOU: Enjoying my summer..no complaints! Though I'm not sure I'd be enjoying it that much if I was in Brooklyn. Lol. By the way I'm George...I take it you're real name is Leah?*

> *LEAH: You'd love it here! No raggedy girls in my neighborhood, I promise. Yep, I'm Leah, nice to meet you George. That's actually my dogs name!*

> *YOU: So what are you trying to say? LOL...So where are you in your main photo? That looks like Puerto Rico*

> *LEAH: Yeah I was there for spring break. OMG I had such a great time.....drank out of coconuts while lying out on the beach every day! Wow you know your places. Been before?*

YOU: Something like that. ;) So other than travel the world, what else do you like to do? You kinda have a cute, obnoxious smile like a cheerleader or something.

LEAH: Close. I used to be in the color guard at my high school! You're silly! And once again, thanks for the compliment (I think!) lol. Other than that, I love the movies, museums and shopping. I need new shoes actually.

YOU: Your welcome, I think. Lol. Well Leah, so far you SEEM like a cool female. I guess time will tell. Let's exchange numbers. My number is 555-5555. Call me tonight around 8.

At this point, *Leah* from our example has a few choices. She may call you as you've instructed which is a great sign. Or she may offer her number and wait for you to call her, which isn't too bad either. If you request that she calls you, and she replies asking you to call her, it may be excusable if she offers a reason. This is normally a defense mechanism women use to try to maintain "control" over the interaction. Look at this as your first test!

PAY ATTENTION TO HER TESTS

As explained above, keep in mind that women will test you. One of the most common tests is to see how much you will bend. A common way women test guys online is to get guys to call them, *after* he has already asked her to call him.

If a woman <u>ignores</u> your request to call you and only leaves her number as a reply to your request, don't take the bait…at least not without her _knowing_ that you're not going to chase her like a dog in heat. As stated under

"Disrespectful Women" in Chapter 3, do not let this go unchecked. If she suggests that you call her after you've requested her to call you, let her know that you're not one to chase females. I suggest being both light-hearted and serious. Something like one of the following would do (keep in mind that both the emoticons and using "lol" takes the edge off your statements):

> -"No thanks but good try. My number is two messages up! ;)"
>
> -"I asked first...you got the number ;)"
>
> -"WRONG ANSWER! Lol. I expect to hear from you at 8!"

If *Leah* from our example uses any excuses—any at all to keep things going online, she is *NOT* interested. Move on. If she keeps the chat going, that is her guilty conscience trying to make herself feel better for not wanting to call you. She might even say, "I need to get to know you better." Fellas, this is womanese for one of the following:

> -*"I already have a man, but may need you just in case."*
>
> -*"I already have a man, but may need you to boost my ego from time to time."*
>
> -*"I want to toy with you and test my desirability."*
>
> -*"I don't know how to reject you and this avoids pain for me."*

I don't care how fine she is. I don't care how much she flirts with you. Moving forward is the *only way* you will get her from Facebook to your blackbook. If she does this, move on. I will expand more on female BS in Chapter 10.

ON THE PHONE AND TO THE DATE

Fellas, once you have her on the phone, the rest should be easy. Keep in mind this does *not* mean you're guaranteed a date. Realize that a lot of women these days "flake" or cancel dates at the last minute at very high rates. My friends and even I have been stood up. No one is immune. **This is why I started with my fellas and wrote *The Facebook Datebook for Men*, first!** Allow me to go on a mini-tangent.

Many women can relate to a time at a very young age when they began talking about male-female relations. Many times, females are very young—most times well before puberty when they first talk about boys and marriage and the idea of love. Women eat up the idea of "relationships". They dominate this genre of books and film. Why do you think they call them "Chick Flicks?" Women understandably have an advantage when it comes to the world of dating.

We fellas, are normally a little late. Very few of us were raised knowing guys who could "lace" us with quality game. Most men out here are directionless. And it isn't our fault—it's simply the breakdown of society. I'm not going to get too deep. However, take these words to heart and it will improve both your offline and online game. Proceed.

With your telephone call, keep the conversation brief—five to ten minutes at most. Return to the familiar conversational topics you had online to get her to feel the same emotions she had earlier. This allows her to connect *to* you a bit more. After a few minutes, suggest a time, date and location to hang out. Keep in mind that you want to hint that your time is limited. This will once again place her mind at ease if she's concerned that she might be stuck with "a guy from the internet." It also makes you seem busy—which is a good thing. Something like this would suffice:

> *You seem like a very cool female…This Thursday I have a few things to do, but let's hang out for a little bit before I head out later on. How's 6:30 at Starbucks?*

Once again, read her response, the same way you did with her messages. No matter the case, **always** have a backup plan for that date and time. You may even want to schedule multiple dates at once. The most humane thing to do is be honest and let your "backup" girls know that you're not sure if you'll be available and offer to call them if you are. As long as you let them know the deal, they should be okay with that. Got it? Good.

For a deeper explanation on first date and phone number rules, peep *The Men's Guide*.

Chapter Five – Crutches and Pitfalls

D ue to the various ways you can contact women on Facebook, it can be down right confusing to figure out which way is best. Just about every feature, in my opinion has it's own purpose. It's all about *tact*. Some ways to initiate contact are better than others, depending on what you want to do. However in this chapter, I will be breaking down the ways you *don't* want to initiate contact.

Here are the five ways **<u>NOT</u>** start off a Facebook interaction:

> 1) Poking
>
> 2) Sending friend invites
>
> 3) Leaving wall comments, especially when you don't know her
>
> 4) Too much messaging
>
> 5) Chatting

Poking

Would you ever walk up to a stranger and poke them? (Hopefully your answer to that question was, "No"). Okay, then poking a stranger online is just as weird.

When I was on The Tyra Banks Show® earlier this year, there was a female guest who complained about receiving pokes from random guys. She was completely freaked out about it and I don't blame her. Poking is lame, when done as a first point of contact. Plenty of women tell me about the random pokes they've received from strangers on Facebook. Unless she's just super attracted to your photo or is just playing around, she will probably not respond to you positively, if at all.

In addition to it being pointless, poking goes against the principle of exuding manhood. When dealing with women for the first time, you want to be direct without showing any fear or hesitation. The same goes for being online. Although pokes aren't all bad (we'll dissect the good uses later in the book), starting out with a poke is not the way to start out. It's just creepy. Don't do it, playas!

Sending Friend Invites

Be honest...do you really *just* want to be her friend? Again, your answer to this question should be "No", if you're honest. Although you want to accomplish the goals of expressing your interest and seeing her full profile (which is normally allowed once you two are Facebook friends), this is normally not the best way to start out.

Similar to poking, sending friend invites to express interest in a female is a very passive way to express your interest. Passiveness will **not** get your foot in the door. To me, *friendquesting* is similar to leaving a "Do You Like Me?" note in her locker in grade school or telling one of her girlfriends that you like her. Most guys do this out of the fear of rejection. Be fearless and direct, fellas! Women are attracted to confidence. Even if she rejects you or doesn't reply, your balls are still in tact. Hold onto your pride!

As you may already know, Facebook allows its users to attach short notes to friend invites. While this is a little better, I do not recommend this, under normal circumstances. Asking her to "be your friend" this soon may give her the sensation of feeling superior to you. While it is acceptable that she expresses interest in you via *friendquesting* you, you should opt to be more direct and engaging, as any man should.

Leaving Wall Comments (without exchanging messages)

In most cases, if you *can* leave a wall comment, you've already been added as a friend. And if your friend invite was your first attempt at contacting her, you already violated the rule above. (If she *friendquests* you first, it is not necessarily *that* bad to leave her a wall comment). Beyond violating the rule against sending a friend invite as a means of first contact, there are other problems with sending a wall comment as well.

First of all, it makes you look weak and places you on display for her friends and girlfriends if you try to get to know her on her wall. This is something I expect my young readers to have done. As I addressed with The Ramiro and Pebbles Morning Show from JAMN 94.5 (you can catch that at http://www.MySpaceToMyPlace.com), leaving public comments will do nothing to help you meet women online. You will not be taken seriously if you attempt to get to know a woman this way. They should be used, instead, for attention-getting purposes. (More on that later in the book).

Excessive Messaging

While messaging is the suggested way to meet women by Facebook, *too much* messaging will kill your chances. This is especially true with your first message. If you send her a message that goes unreturned for a few days, do **not** follow up with another message to "make sure she got it." Fellas, she got it! And if she didn't reply, move on! I'll be damned if you're going to buy this book and become a bug-a-boo. They are going to be stalking *you* by the time I'm done with you!

Anyway, once you've captured a female's interest and built a certain degree of comfort with her, you must get her to the phone…quickly. A good rule of thumb is to keep it to under eight exchanges. If you've exchanged more than ten messages with a woman you met through Facebook, resolve yourself to the fact that you two have established an "internet relationship" and will probably never meet in real life, unless you stalk her. This is not recommended!

The more you message her, the less intrigue you will maintain and the more you will box yourself into the category as her Facebook friend. Don't do it to yourself. Keep it short and sweet and carry the interaction forward!

Chatting Way Too Soon

In Chapter 9, I will explain how you can use the Facebook Chat feature to your advantage to speed up your interactions with women on Facebook. Until then, I do not recommend chatting it up with a new prospect. For a moment, imagine you are a female getting a chat request from some random guy you accepted a friend invite from. It's downright *creepy*. Making women comfortable is a big part of your online game. Start slowly, but quickly and smoothly progress the online interaction! Save the chatting for later!

In addition to the common interaction mistakes guys make above, there are a few other pitfalls that you must avoid when continuing a message exchange. Here are some things you must stay clear from:

IDLE CONVERSATION

You will never meet a female from Facebook or any other site if you do not know how to guide a conversation. I hate to break it to you fellas, but this is **your** responsibility. In every normal interaction with a female, you need to be the "captain of conversation."

Idle chatter often occurs when you're either thinking too hard or not thinking enough. When you're thinking too hard, you are often overanalyzing what is being said instead of *how* it is being said. When that happens, you spend too much time trying to structure things perfectly. When I used to do this, my chats appeared scripted which quickly killed my game. There is no "perfect" conversation—it should always appear unscripted. You need to have the ability to take any reply and turn it into an interesting response. More on this later.

On the flipside, idle chatter can result from not thinking hard enough. For instance, most guys do not read everything on a woman's profile, if anything. However, if you are on your second or third exchange and start to ask questions, you may want to at least skim through her profile. If not, she may dismiss and disqualify you because you didn't even bother to read her page. Here's a secret fellas: *most times, all of what you need to know about a woman is already on her profile page.* Many times they don't even realize this. Think smart and think ahead of the conversation and you will tip the odds of getting her from "Facebooking" to your place, cooking!

PHYSICAL COMMENTS AND COMPLIMENTS

This is another by product of simply not thinking. **You do not need to compliment a woman on her appearance to win brownie points.** Forget that. Women know how good they look—especially when it comes to her photos. Do you think she chose her photos on accident? Heck no. She *knows* she looks good in that photo. I would put money down that dozens of guys have already complimented her beauty in that very same photograph you are staring at. And if you do the same, you'll be nothing to her but a "pick-me-up" and ego-booster. If you'd rather raise her spirits than her skirt, keep complimenting her eyes, her face, and breasts. But if you'd rather give her more reasons to respect you, save the brown-nosing compliments for the next dude.

SEXUAL LANGUAGE

This *should* be common sense. However, let's be clear—no matter how *ho-ish* or scandalous a woman may appear (or actually be), do not get sexual online. Even if she brings it up, it's best to dismiss it by smoothly changing the conversation. I've personally had a few women make overt sexual references in terms of what she'd like to do with me to which I've responded, "Time will tell" or "We'll see if you can 'back it up'". Whatever the case, do not get sucked in to getting sexual online. Many women will use this as a test to see how easily you are thrown off your mackin.   Don't fall for it and do not get excited. Although they may not acknowledge it, women notice how cool you will come across and it will present yourself as even more of a challenge.

That said, congrats for making it to the midway part of the book. Get up, stretch, send a note or two and come back. I'll be here.

On to the good stuff ;)

Chapter Six – War Tactics

To be a good "netmack", it is vital to know how to shift a woman's attention. As we discussed earlier, there are a variety of ways to make your profile "pop out". Yet I've found that nothing gets a woman's attention like…what else: *another* woman!

I sort of learned this by accident. While dating a woman (that I actually met through Facebook), a platonic female friend of mine left a compliment on my wall about my profile picture. My girl saw the comment and posted a comment about how she thought I looked better in another picture. The platonic friend went on to point out how much she liked my outfit, to which my girl made a comment about seeing me later on that day. That evening, and for a few days following, I noticed that my girl tried much harder to earn my affection. It became abundantly clear that I was merely a prop in a "wall war". Sweet!

WHY WOMEN COMPETE

As much as we might like to *think* that women get "dolled up" for us guys when they hit the social scene, we must be realistic. Fellas, it's not for us. We are not the primary focus of all the preening women do when they hit the clubs and social spots. *They* are the reason. And not in a lesbian kind of way either. Women are in competition with *each other*. When women look at each other, they often find themselves making physical comparisons. This phenomenon is the undertone which controls the overall mood in a particular venue. The competitive nature amongst women is so deep, it is often the reason why best friends often find themselves competing over a man:

> *Women are so busy competing with each other for male attention that they do not have the psychological, intellectual or emotional insight to change the social climate that is causing them to suffer from low-self esteem. Women think of men as being promiscuous, unfaithful, lying, cheating dogs. But what*

most women need to come to grips with and understand is that
research shows that a man is most likely to have a sexual affair
with a woman's best friend, relative or neighbor... a woman
whom she trusts, loves and respects. One of the reasons that
men who cheat are so successful at it is because women allow
them to because they are in competition with each other. [7]

Having dated and kicked it with many attractive women, I
personally believe that the *more* attractive a woman is, the more
difficult it is for her to have good friends. In that same token,
the cuter she is, the less friends she tends to have. As they say,
"It's lonely at the top".

Below are eight reasons given by psychologist, Cassandra G.
Sturges on why women "hate" each other:

1. Women feel that their biological prime-time is limited. She can
easily be replaced by a new younger, more beautiful woman. Youth is
a woman's fair-weathered friend.

2. Women feel that other women control their man's sexual fidelity.

3. Women feel that their level or degree of physical beauty is based on
luck as opposed to something that she controls.

4. Women feel that other women can take something that they have
worked hard to earn by using their beauty on the job, school and the
legal system because men will be taken by her beauty.

5. Women feel that other women can not be trusted. They gossip too
much, they are phony and they would take your man right before your
eyes.

6. Women feel that other women divert attention away from them.

7. Women feel psychologically competitive with other women to be
more attractive.

---

[7] Sturges, Cassandra George. "Why Women Hate Other Women." E-Zine Articles. May 21,
2007. http://ezinearticles.com/?Why-Women-Hate-Other-Women&id=573904.

8. Women subconsciously believe that if they merely looked like another woman, they could inherit her life, her diamond, her man, and people would look at her with the same admiration.[8]

HOW THIS BENEFITS YOU

So what does this have to do with you? More importantly, how does waging a "wall war" help your cause? The answer is, it helps *tremendously*. When multiple women are competing over your wall, you are getting more shine—from *other* women. And the more women that join in, the better. But even if you don't have any additional takers, rest assured that many are watching. In the meantime, they are checking out your photos. If your appearance is "crispy" and clean as I described in Chapter One, you are well on your way to receiving messages, "pokes" and friend requests as a result.

WAYS TO PROVOKE A WAR

Now that you know the benefits of hosting a wall war, how do you create one? What should you do? As you begin to improve your profile and start your search, you will notice a change in the way females respond. If done right, women should be more friendly and engaging overall. Your online game should see some improvements. That in itself lays the groundwork for some catfights over your online attention. Next, I will explain the ways to get the comments rolling.

STEP ONE: Lay the Groundwork: *Update your status, mentioning a Facebook Friend*

Every time you meet a new, attractive lady—say at a bar or a club—get her Facebook information. (Facebook now allows

---

[8] Sturges, Cassandra George. "Why Women Hate Other Women." E-Zine Articles. May 21, 2007. http://ezinearticles.com/?Why-Women-Hate-Other-Women&id=573904.

users to choose their own unique web address or "URL"). Make sure you build a good rapport with these women—even if it's on a platonic level. Your goal is to "stockpile" sexy women who will be your advocates—even though they don't know it. Once you have a few women, casually mention one of them in a Facebook update, in a way that will provoke a friendly and/or flirtatious reply. This will get you noticed and will increase your desirability.

The key is, you want to do this soon after this Facebook Friend has recently changed something on her profile. That way you know that she is more likely to return sometime again in the near future. If she is a casual Facebook user, this will not work!

For instance, say you met an attractive woman named Stacy Green at a lounge but she was only in town for the weekend from another state. You get Stacy's Facebook information and correspond with her a few times through email (As we've already explained in Chapter Three, long distance mackin is *not* recommended! However you *can* use her as bait!)

Once a good rapport is built with Stacy, she is now prepped. If she changes her profile picture you can update your status with something like:

Looking at Stacy Green's new profile pic. So business-like ;)

Keep in mind that this was **not** a physical compliment, nor was it "simpish", meaning brown-nosing. If done with good timing, Stacy will reply to your update, which will appear on your wall and visible to all of your friends through your newsfeed. You may not see anyone else join your playful dialogue, but Females *will* take note.

Do not be discouraged if you are rusty at first—it takes timing and relies on her attention span. Once you've repeated this step with a few ladies, you are now ready for step two.

Note: You may choose instead to comment on one of her photos or on *her* status, instead of updating *your* status. Yet, while she is more likely to see your comment, you will be reaching her circle of friends, rather than yours. If this isn't your goal, you should choose to update your own status.

STEP TWO: Make an open invitation, "The Tigger Approach"

Once you've lured a couple of attractive women to comment on your status, realize that you're being watched a little more closely. Other women in your network (if your profile is visible) or at least on your friends list will likely take an interest or at least be curious about your next move. This is when you use "The Tigger Approach".

I am calling this "The Tigger Approach" to give credit to a friend of mined, nicknamed "Tigger". He has this down to a science and we've always laughed about how something so simple could be so effective. All you need to do is make an open invitation for one of your lady friends to do something for you. Here are some common examples of status updates, both Tigger and I have used (using the name "John Smith"):

> ***John Smith*** *is having neck pain. Wishing it was rubbed.*
> ***John Smith*** *just wants a good meal right about now.*
> ***John Smith*** *wouldn't mind company later on.*

Realize that none of these updates pleaded for attention nor do they make you appear desperate. Make sure you use language that provokes a reaction, yet doesn't convey weakness.

If you have followed STEP ONE correctly, a few ladies will likely respond to your "Tigger"/open invitation status update. This can easily turn into a war as women may start competing for your attention. Keep in mind that this is normally just flirting.

So why do it? **Number one, it will make it easier for you to mack to other women on your friends list, and secondly, it will give women more reason to express interest in you via a poke, friend request, or message.**

Hopefully by now you've realized why this is "STEP TWO". If "STEP ONE" is skipped, you run the risk of looking lame if no one replies to your open invitation. Do not risk it. Make sure STEP ONE is repeated until you have it down pat.

STEP THREE: Relax and watch

Okay, I admit: there is no step three! It's literally this simple. As explained earlier, women can be very competitive which makes for an interesting wall war. Here's an example of a wall war, where "Jane Johnson" is insistent on getting some attention. (Note that John chimes in on his own wall to acknowledge the ladies).

<u>Your status message</u>:
John Smith *is having neck pain. Wishing it was rubbed.*

Status Comments:

Jane Johnson I've been know for my massage skills ;)

Keisha Stewart You know I'm not far away!

Ashley Cho Oh poor baby! :(

John Smith My neck is starting to feel better already :-D

Jane Johnson Did I mention I was taking physical therapy classes? ;)

John Smith Oh really…maybe I'll have to take you up on that.

Jane Johnson Maybe you should :)

It may not look like much, but realize that both "Keisha Stewart" and "Ashley Cho" saw what was going on. It is very likely that others saw it too. Once you begin to do this every so often, it will make it much easier to "pluck" women from Facebook and put them into your blackbook!

Chapter Seven – "Whoring" Yourself

U p until now I've used the term "whoring" (attention-whoring) in a somewhat negative context. This is because of the provocative behavior many young women use to satisfy their desire to be noticed by men. As a result many guys are disillusioned into believing they "have a chance" with a woman, when in reality, he doesn't stand a chance. It's time to tip the scales in your favor, fellas.

NEWS FEED

As you probably already know, Facebook has a mechanism which allows its users to see an ongoing snapshot of all the happenings within his or her friends. This means that many of your actions, such as leaving comments on photos and adding friends can be seen by your Facebook friends. The place where these updates are seen is called the Facebook News Feed and had been a controversial addition when it was first introduced. Many Facebook users found it invasive and obnoxious. Yet it seems to have been embraced and Facebook continues to increase its membership at a rapid pace. Overall, it seems like most of its users have accepted the "News Feed"

Knowing how to master the news feed is important, fellas. Similar to waging a "wall war", the goal of whoring yourself is to help elevate your status on Facebook. It is no secret that females are generally more attracted to popular men. This explains the scores of women who chase athletes, entertainers and even businessmen. These women, better known as groupies, enjoy the thrill of the chase and the idea of being around someone popular.

Well fellas, now it's your turn. The quickest, most effective way to reach "celebrity status" in your Facebook network is to show off. How? I'm glad you asked.

Keep status messages interesting and funny

Everybody likes to be entertained, right? Thanks to status messages, Facebook allows you a chance to take center stage—at least for a split second while your status remains new and fresh. Now, I'm not saying that your goal is to be a stand-up comedian, but displaying little tidbits of wit can go a long way. Let's say for instance, you decide to take a trip to the zoo. You could make an update like, "Going to the zoo today...planning to hold my breath the ENTIRE time." It always helps if you have the Facebook application on your phone, as it allows you to make updates from anywhere. If you are not sure what updates to use, you can literally google for "funny Facebook status messages." It goes a long way!

Share interesting news or articles

If you happen to come across an interesting news report or a Youtube® link, definitely post or "share" the link. Unless you are posting things every five minutes, it's almost impossible to do this *too* often—just make sure it is thought provoking enough. My suggestion is to find things that generate a reaction.

For instance a few weeks back, I ran into an article which claimed that a study proved that women were more attracted to men already in relationships. I titled the link, "women are so dirty! ;) " and my comment wall became littered with replies. As stated earlier, having a lot of ladies visit your page is always a positive thing, especially if your profile is in order. Most of these women will scan your photos and check you out. You may even get a "poke" or friend request from these ladies, which indicates interest. Even if you cannot find an interesting story from a news website, you can always do a search for "interesting facts" and post a link. The possibilities are endless.

Ask questions that will generate strong reaction

You want to be careful with this one fellas—do not get women pissed at you! Asking questions like, "Why are women so overweight?" probably will not get you very far. Your goal is to keep your question light, while still grabbing her attention. Throwing in a little sarcasm or humor always helps! Questions like, "why does it seem like women are only after one thing? ;)" work because it is something normally said by a woman about guys, rather than what a guy may say about women. Similar with sharing interesting news and articles, make sure your question is thought provoking!

OTHER WAYS TO "WHORE" YOURSELF

Take your camera *everywhere*

You *never* know when you'll see something interesting. That's why it is key that you always have a camera on you—at least a camera phone. When at all possible, invest in a small, digital camera which takes crystal clear photos. When you're at the museum, the park or better yet, at special events such as concerts, you want to have a camera on you. Undoubtedly, bringing the camera with you on vacation is a *must*. You will appear worldly—even if you only hop a plane once every couple of years.

As stated before, appearing in photographs with other cute women will increase your stock value tremendously. Do not let an opportunity pass when you bump into or meet a pretty female. Give a passerby your camera and get a quick picture. That will be your bait to reel in "plenty of fish" on Facebook!

Tagging

If you do not already know, "tagging" is term meaning to let Facebook know exactly who is in a picture. This is done by clicking on the person (normally their face), and inserting that person's name. Tagging goes hand in hand with taking your camera everywhere, since many of these photos will include you, along with other people. The beauty in tagging is that if you tag a cute lady who also has a Facebook page, you will likely be seen by both your friends and hers or even her networks (depending on her account settings). This simply increases your "whoredom" which, again, is your strong suit. And if you can, be sure to tag a celebrity or two if you can get a picture with him or her. Yes, I know I sound like a groupie. So, who cares? I'm not suggesting that you follow Beyonce's Tour Bus. Yet if you run into someone, take a photo with them, find their Facebook page and tag them!

There are instances when tagging can go wrong. While I was a guest on the Tyra Banks Show®, there was another guest who was on the show for this reason. While she was at a party, she was pressured by her friends to dance on stage. Although she was hesitant given her short dress, she agreed and participated. A day or two later, she logged into her Facebook account to find scores of comments on a photo—an "up-skirt photo" of her taken by a guy at the party! She was devastated. Fellas, I do not expect you to throw on a skirt anytime soon—at least I hope not! However, be mindful of your actions at all times. As technology gets more sophisticated, realize that you can be blasted all over the internet within seconds!

To remedy this, I suggest having Facebook notify you if someone should tag your photo. To do this go to your "Account Settings" and select "Notifications." This will allow you to "approve" the tag before it happens and would have surely alerted the lady mentioned above about her infamous tag!

In the meantime, tell your friends to show you the picture or at least alert you before they decide to blast you all over cyberspace!

Be a clown (every once and a while)

Every now and then, it is cool to be silly. I would say that randomly—3 to 4 times a year—post a silly picture of yourself in your main photo. A good example is going to a site which manipulates your photo to make it appear that you have a 50's yearbook photo. Never be afraid to experiment with this one, guys. Women love guys with no boundaries and one who shows spirit. Display that!

WHORING IS YOUR FRIEND

In short, always be willing to be creative and distinguish yourself. If you begin heeding to just *some* of the advice in this chapter it will become second nature. And once the women start rolling in, you'll have to beat them off with a stick!

Chapter Eight – Honesty Mackin'

This is, by far, one of my favorite subjects and is how I've met many women, including an ex-girlfriend. Fellas, I'm about to lace you up with some serious game! Do you hear me? Proceed, playas!

Since joining Facebook a few years ago, nothing made me more excited than the Honesty Box application. This application allows you to anonymously message anyone on your friends list—the only thing they know and see about you is your gender. The intrigue in using this, by itself, is enough to pique the curiosity of anyone. By personal experience, women are fascinated with strangers...at least strangers who effectively use this application.

Where to begin

I tend to only use Honesty Box when I really don't know the person too well—or at least someone I haven't spoke with in years. Let's say you come across a cute female who went to your high school a few years back and now lives in your city. Instead of messaging her right away, you could request her as a friend. This isn't the most direct approach, yet it accomplishes three things: 1) you see if she's at least *interested enough* to accept your friend request, 2) it will allow you access to her profile, pictures and information, and 3) it gets her to thinking about you on some level. Once she is your friend, all you need to do is wait.

Why wait? And how long? Obviously if you friend request her and send her an honesty box message, she will likely suspect you, as the originator. Where's the fun and mystery in that? My suggestion is to wait at least one week before sending her an honesty box message. Normally I advocate for moving her off the internet quickly. However, in situations where you know someone from your past, I think a more careful approach should be taken. See fellas, when women already know you (or know *of* you), their opinion of you is already set. It's very difficult to change her impression of you. As they say, first impressions are lasting. Honesty Box is your key to helping her reshape her opinion of you.

The week or longer waiting period isn't all bad, as you can still get at other females. If you've been following the principles in chapters one through seven, you'll have a steady supply of women from Facebook anyway. Once at least seven days has passed, it's time to pounce on her like a lion on an innocent lamb!

Your first "HB" (Honesty Box) message

Given it has been multiple years since you two have last spoken or seen each other, this makes her "ripe" to be *honesty macked*. Assuming she's available, your first step is to analyze her profile. How does she measure up? You need to identify your prospect as we discussed in Chapter 3. Is she a SLOPE or POKE woman? More specifically is she "bougie" or shy? Knowing this information will help guide you with your first message.

No matter her type, one thing that links my HB messages together is their bluntness. Many women, who otherwise would be offended, are more intrigued when they get blunt anonymous messages. Why? Well humans are curious creatures and perhaps the mystery makes it more alluring. Who knows? The bottom line is you want to appeal to her emotions of wanting to be swept away by a "bad boy." Yes, fellas—time to turn it on and be what you are: a man.

In that first message, make an observation and turn it into a flirtatious message. Say she's a freak you haven't seen or spoken to since high school. Compliment her on something physical, but add flair. Say something like, "Damn…you've grown up since high school. 36Cs, I'm guessing?" If she's the shy, good girl type, say something like, "You've always had the shy, sexy thing going on. Wouldn't mind seeing what that's about." Your goal in the first note is to observe her "type" and to turn it up a notch.

HB Conversation Flow

That said, I prefer to leave the four letter f- word out of it, along with unnecessary cursing. I like to use the word, "bang". Also make sure you do **not** ask direct questions—only give suggestions. Seem selfish. Act like rapper/hip hop mogul P. Diddy—as if every female is a planet revolving around you, the sun. Be alluring. Most of all, **never** tell her who you are until you get her phone number. I personally find it fascinating how a female who has **no idea** who you are will tell you the most intimate things about herself in an HB conversation. You can learn her inner most secrets, whether she has a man, if he's "hitting it" right, etc. And remember fellas, no matter *how offended* she may pretend to be, chances are she is intrigued by you if she keeps talking to you.

Explaining how to flow in an exchange is most easily defined in this example (using the freaky girl approach):

YOU: Damn…you've grown up since high school. 36Cs, I'm guessing?

HER: Ummm…wow…who is this?

YOU: Jackpot. I knew I was dead on the money.

HER: *Actually I'm a 34C. Close. Who are you?*

YOU: *C'mon that would take away the fun of Honesty Box. So when was the last time you "got some?"*

HER: *Hmmm, its been a while. So you know me from high school, huh? Were we in the same homeroom?*

YOU: *Like I'm going to tell you. You always seemed like the shy, lonely type. Usually those are the worst ones ;)*

HER: *Worst ones? How?*

YOU: *What do you think?*

HER: *LOL!!! WHO IS THIS??? Just tell me who you are!!!*

YOU: *I want to meet up, sit down over a coffee and then take you back to my place bang you. Wear a skirt. What are you doing Friday?*

HER: *Tell me who you are FIRST.*

YOU: *Number? I'll call you at 9:45.*

HER: *555-2469*

Fellas, don't ever make Honesty Box complicated! Your main rule is to never reveal who you are until you get her number.

And if she pressures, keep the conversation going with a sly reply, and a vague sexual reference or question. When she cannot stand it, end with a statement saying that you want to meet up for something simple (like coffee, ice cream, a walk in the park, etc), and that you'd like to do something to her. (You can even say, "I want to do something to you.") Suggest a day and demand her number. If it doesn't work. Move on. She doesn't know who you are anyway! No harm done!

Okay I have her number! Now what?!

You call!!! That's what you do. However, keep the mystery going and your call blocked (*67 in most cases). If she doesn't pick up, wait a few days and tease her some more on Honesty Box about her being "slow." If she picks up, she may or may not recognize your voice. Probably not. On the phone, keep playing with her. Ask her questions. Get into her brain. Then once this is done, you have to move to the part you cannot control—her reaction to who you really are.

Here's when it gets shaky. Fellas, you nor I have *any* control over her reaction once she finds out who you are. It helps if she liked you or was at least neutral to you in high school. Chances are, if she thought you were a "herb" (geek) back then, then those "herbal" feelings may return. If she receives you well, simply set up a date, time and location to meet—preferably in the following 1-3 days for coffee. To make yourself seem less "hungry", *invite* her out (don't ask) and let her know that if you two hang out, she has to make sure she looks *good* since she's with you. Say it with a smile in your voice. Tease her. Become the type of dude that girls have to fight over. If you do this right, you *will* become him! It's a beautiful thing!

When you two meet for the first time, play it cool. Act like superman. Listen to some inspiring music on your iPod or in the car on your way to see her. In a way, you represent something exciting to her. Go with it.

Fellas, you may want to read and re-read this chapter. I've pulled some quality women with this knowledge, including my ex, who I happen to think is still a great catch—just a little too crazy.

To get this application, you can simply run a Facebook search for "Honesty Box." Have fun!

Chapter Nine – Speed Mackin' UNLEASHED

I f you read *The Men's Guide*, then you are already familiar with the concept of "Speed Mackin'". For those who don't know, Speed Mackin' is the art of getting a woman from the internet to an in-person meeting within hours or even minutes! However, I am going to expand on this concept and give you guys some more tips on how to accomplish this even more easily than in my first book. Sit back and learn from the mack!

Why SPEED is your friend

There are a variety of reasons why SPEED is your friend, guys. As most macks already know, women tend to project their fantasies onto a man when they first meet. This is also the root reason behind what many deem as the "honeymood period." Things usually always seem pleasant at first. You want to strike when *you* are still the new guy to her. That means between your first note and your first meet-up, less than a day, or even an hour has passed. And fellas, I've done this so much, I've lost count!

Personally, I'm an impatient individual. I have cancelled dates within the first few minutes of getting there, simply because I already know things aren't going to turn out the way I like. And if I see a cute lady online, I *want* to see her soon. Don't you?

Speed is also your friend because it lets her know that you are an assertive "go-getter." While men are increasingly becoming more effeminate, women are assuming more positions of power in society. Therefore becoming a more assertive and straightforward type of guy will work to your advantage, simply because it's rare.

How do you begin to Speed Mack?

That's just it—you begin to speed mack just like any other interaction. Find her type. If she's a "SLOPE" or "POKE" girl, then proceed. If not, drop her.

Next, is she a total stranger? Begin with a regular message exchange, as described earlier. Else, you could go with the "HB" approach if this is someone from your past. Either way, get her going for about 1 or 2 exchanges. So what's different about the "speed" approach? It's all about chance *and* seizing the opportunity.

Is she online?

Fellas, the Speed Mackin' approach will *only* work if she is online at the time. To find out, find out when she sent you a note. In fact, notice her patterns. If she sends you notes and updates her page around the same times throughout the day, then that is the time you need to "just happen" to be online. Another way to discover her pattern is to remain "Active" on your chat box. See that chat area on the lower right-hand portion of your screen? Keep an eye on that. If you remain active, you can also see your friends who are active.

Seizing the opportunity

Say you've exchanged a message or two (or 3 or 4) with a female and you see that she's online. Double click her name in the chat box. You're now ready to speed mack her off Facebook! Warning: I do **not** normally suggest chatting with a female you haven't exchanged any messages with. Similar to poking, it's weird and your probability of successfully speed mackin' her is not high.

Once the chat window is open, begin your chat.

Speed mackin' flow

It's okay to start with a "hi" or "hello", but I suggest following up with some personality. If it's late at night, a slick remark might be, "Isn't it past your bedtime? ;)" (Don't forget the emoticon!)

If you can incorporate something you two have already discussed in a message exchange, then that's even better. Say you two already talked about how short she is, then a cute first message would be, "Isn't it past your bedtime, *little girl*? ;)" Whatever the case your objective is *speed*. You absolutely must get her on the phone within 20 minutes at most, though I prefer to do this in under 10-15 minutes. Conduct your chat the same way you would a message exchange, but spend more time on each component.

Here is a **general** guide for speed mackin':

First 5-7 minutes – Small talk; how she's been, what her life is like these days

Next 2-3 minutes – Her recent activities, current happenings in her life, the status quo

Final 3-5 minutes – Her plans for the next couple of days

Now fellas, I do **not** want you to follow the time allotment perfectly. Sometimes it happens more quickly than other times. Yet keep this in mind and use it as a guide!

Now it is time to put on your fatigues and go to war. The mission is never easy at first and may take some getting used to. But men, it will get easier. If you pay attention you *will* enjoy some success. Here is your mission, if you choose to accept it!

"Shoot the breeze" – Target time: 5 minutes

Begin the chat with small talk. Find out how she's been and how she feels about life, in general. Your main goal here is to make her feel comfortable and to get her talking. Keep in mind that many women will talk your ear off once you've asked the magical question, "How do you feel?" Take advantage!

Current Events – Target time: 2 minutes

Midway into how she feels, find out some tangible things she's done recently. If she hasn't done much, expand on this. Ask her where she's been in the world. Then ask her what those places were like. Act interested and curious. Expand this into what she likes to do and what she wants out of life. As she answers these questions, she is providing you with more potential questions and thought provoking responses. Keep a "wit" about you and use it from time to time. For instance, if she says that she loves to see "romantic comedies", tell her that she sounds like a typical, "chick-flick"-loving female. Make sure you use a winking emoticon! This allows her to build trust in you because unlike most guys you do not appear to be overly concerned about her reactions. (On that note, never agree with her 100% of the time. Get her to see things from your perspective.)

Setting her up – Target time: 3 minutes

We've now come to the point where we start to close out the speed mackin' conversation. Spend some time asking her about her future plans for the coming days. Do not ask about a specific day—i.e. "What are you doing Saturday?" That sounds too much like you're asking her out. And that's *not* something you do online! However you want her to start **thinking** about it. A better question is, "So what are your plans over the next coming week? What's your schedule like?" Regardless of her answer, seem interested and allow her to expand. While she's talking, take mental notes of the days she seems overly occupied or busy with work, school, activities, etc. Allow your mind to become curious about her "happenings" and invite her to share more. Got it? Good.

It's time. FIRE!

At this point you should have a good handle on her schedule. Ready to get it done?

In the middle of her ranting about her upcoming plans, interrupt her and let her know you have to get offline. However, have her call you within 20 minutes. Your exchange at this point should look like this,

YOU: *Damn! I gotta get offline. You seem like a cool female though! Do me a favor….*

HER: *You seem cool too…what's that?*

YOU: *Give me a call in exactly 5 minutes: 555-8984. And when you call, don't try to sound super-sexy. ;)*

HER: *Lol. Okay.*

"What ifs"

Here are some common, "What ifs" which may occur from time to time.

What if she tells me to call her instead? What does this mean?

Basically she is either uninterested or is testing you. "Pass the test" by addressing this immediately. For more, revisit Chapter 4.

What if she doesn't reply after I've left my number?

She probably has a man and only uses Facebook to garner attention. Nothing personal. Move on.

What if she never calls? Or what if she continues to keep the chat going?

She's not interested or at least, not interested enough. Move on. You might even want to tell her that you will talk to her offline. Otherwise, it was nice meeting her. This shows strength and women tend to respond positively to this type of response. I call this a "man-timatum." ;)

What if she calls way beyond the time I requested?

She's testing you. Fellas address this. When this happens, playfully tell her that you're sleepy—even if it's 3PM in the afternoon. Or you can tell her that you missed a birthday while waiting for her. Exaggerate her tardy call and let her know she has to make it up to you. I'll get to that part in a minute!

The transition to the phone…and to the date

At this point, she'll either call or she won't. If you've done your homework, there is a good likelihood she will call out of curiosity. If she doesn't call, or even if she calls beyond that time period, she is not interested or at least, *not interested enough*. In any event, this helps you know where you stand.

Once you are on the phone with her, return to some of the same themes in the chat and "seal the deal" as described in Chapter 4.

If she called late, tease her about it and let her know that she has to make it up to you. Suggest a shoulder rub, a cooked meal, a night at the movies, or something on that level. Act playful, yet ambiguous. This lets her know that you aren't the type of guy to be tested. She must respect your "flyness!"

Here's an example of a valiant speed macking attempt, where she just wasn't interested enough!

ME: interesting page
HER: thanks
ME: who said it was a compliment?
ME: ;)
HER: i like to turn heads…well in this case eyes
HER: u did u just didn't say it
ME: LOL!
ME: smart ass too huh?
HER: not all the time
HER: ima a nice girl
ME: its cool to see an in-shape chick who happens not to seem retarded
ME: how was your day?
HER: it was good urs?
ME: good
ME: what position
ME: do you play?
(a slight sexual innuendo, which doubled as a question about her being a basketball player)

HER: forward
ME: power forward?
HER: im pretty short but i have "ups" lol
HER: yup
ME: cool
ME: can you dunk?
HER: nah nothing like that lol
(Long pause)

ME: i see. i missed a birthday on that last reply. sleepy?
HER: kindof
HER: I'm going to call it a nite
ME: :|
(straight face)

ME: thought you were an athlete
HER: i just came from the gym
HER: i was shooting for 2hours
ME: hopefully you didnt build a house with all those bricks

HER: lol i wasn't lol

ME: I gotcha though
ME: your name?
ME: I'm Flyness by the way
HER: nice to meet u Flyness im Lyla
ME: Awww cute name
ME: LIE-LAAAA

HER: well ok I guess you can pronounce it like that
ME: You know what I'd like?
HER: what do u like?
ME: wait...what are you doing RIGHT now
ME: (besides nodding off)
HER: about to log off and take a shower
HER: y?
ME: when you get out, I want you to call me
ME: and tell me goodnite.
ME: (but dont try to sound all extra sexy)
ME: ;)
ME: 555-1826
HER: wait now lol
HER: are u single?
ME: nope, married with 24 kids
HER: lmao
ME: what do you think?
HER: oh ok
HER: give me ur number
ME: i already did
ME: look up
HER: I might just call you tomorrow
ME: bad answer
HER: well in that case I wont call. lol
ME: Lyla...20 minutes
ME: enjoy your shower ;)

Although the game was good, she was already sleepy, which
forced me to "put up or shut up" and speed up the interaction

---

more quickly than normal. She never called, yet I came out like a champion.

Here's a successful "speed mackin'" story from a female I had exchanged a message with online. Being experienced with meeting females online, I knew she was a shy, freaky, intelligent girl all rolled into one. This chat shows how quickly you can "turn things up." This is somewhat recent so I took some time to hide lot of "identifying information":

ME: hey you
ME: Are you Columbian for real? 100%?
HER: yea y
ME: weird...i met one on here last night
HER: lol
ME: she was saying how she's never met any other Columbians in the US in the last 10 years
HER: where she from
HER: wat state
ME: Austin, TX
ME: enough about her though...she was cute...but not my type
HER: lol ight
ME: how long have you been here?
ME: or were you born here?
HER: nah been here like 6 years now
ME: oh okay. well, welcome anyway ;)
HER: lol thanks
ME: so you're really 20?
HER: yea
ME: sorry looking at your pics
HER: my bday was last week
ME: happy belated babe
HER: thanks
ME: so you work at the hair shop?
HER: weekends only
ME: cool
ME: i see two pictures of you in there with two different outfits on
ME: lol
HER: yea i know. its so boring at times
ME: lol!

ME: how tall are u?
HER: 5'6

(brief pause)
ME: oh sorry...im here staring at your pics............I'm *Flyness* by the way
ME: i love your height

HER: Rachel nice to meet you
HER: why do you like my height?
ME: your legs look long
HER: should i take dat as a compliment?
ME: LOL. ur not a giraffe or anything ;)
ME: yes you should....
HER: ok thank u
ME: i wouldn't mind doing something to you
ME: GOOD...that is
HER: okkk?????
ME: no...nothing crazy
ME: LOL!!! I dont do Voodoo or anything
HER: elaborate plz
ME: sure?
ME: okay well...
ME: i wouldn't mind seeing a movie w/ u...i've been at that theater
downtown before.....
ME: and after the movie....
ME: going to a park...kickin it with you...
ME: maybe swing on the swings...u on my lap
ME: and put you up against a tree...sucking on your neck
ME: turning you around...
ME: wait...my bad
HER: lol
ME: i should just say "ur cute" right?
HER: yea
ME: fuck that
ME: lol
HER: its ok
ME: im assuming ur single....u are?
HER: yea
ME: what are you doing tomorrow night?
HER: sleepin
ME: not making plans with you YET...u gotta pass the crazy test
HER: crazy test???
ME: to make sure u dont stab me. i know a few south american women
who are VICIOUS! lol
ME: Columbians are new to me

HER: wow you're crazy!!! :)
ME: call me right now
ME: 555-1826

Fellas, not only did she call, but we hung out the next day. My planning "worked." And everything up until now has prepared you to do the same. May the force be with you!

Chapter Ten – Other Tips

N ow we are at the final chapter and you may have noticed there's not much left to this book. However, these final few pages are important! They are key! I know you want to get started with "Facebook Mackin'" (and probably already have), but you will, at some point, run into some of these issues!

This chapter is for all of the miscellaneous things you should keep in mind, additional tidbits of information and how to handle some problems.

THE THREE DON'Ts

1. **Don't always show yourself as "available" in the chatbox**

2. **Don't comment on her photos if you're interested**

3. **Don't reply to her message *too* quickly if she doesn't reply to yours quick enough**

DON'T #1: Don't always show yourself as "available" in Facebook chat

Guys, this is not a good move, especially if you are a habitual Facebook user. You always want to appear like you have a life outside of Facebook, even if you use it on your phone. If a lady sees that you are always *on*, it can be a turn *off*. Be mindful of this! When online, rarely allow other users to know!

DON'T #2: Don't comment on her photos if you're interested

This is a mistake most guys make. We often accuse women of being emotional (and they are), but this is an instance where guys completely allow their emotions to get the best of them. I don't care how good she looks in her short shorts. I don't care how smooth her skin is, or how supple her breasts appear. Do **not** leave a compliment. None. Zero. If this is done, she will internalize it as an ego boost and will likely dismiss you as a typical guy who finds her attractive. She will probably find you less attractive and beneath her beauty. Leave the brown-nosing comments alone. They do you no good!

DON'T #3: Don't reply to her message *too* quickly if she doesn't reply to yours quick enough

In other words, guys—don't seem like the "hungry dog" if she's acting like a "cool cat." If she takes 2 days to reply to your notes, take at least that long to reply to hers. Imagine what she would think about a guy who replies to her notes the moment she hits the "send" button. Not cool. Act as if you have a life. Shut down the computer. (Or at least log into another website!)

VACATION MACKIN'

As you already know, the reason why we go on vacation is simple. Girls, girls, girls. As far as I'm concerned, there is no vacation without pretty women. That said, you can use Facebook to your advantage. How do you do this? The way Facebook (or any other social networking site) can help is by providing you with the locals that will be in the area you are vacationing in. Yep—long distance mackin'. (Until you get there, that is!)

Simply put, there are three steps to Vacation Mackin':

1) Scout
2) Friend
3) Exchange

Step one is to scout for females who live at the destination you plan to travel to. About 2-4 weeks before your departure to wherever you choose to travel, search for ladies in the network of that place.

Step two is to "friend" her. As opposed to sending her a message, I prefer adding her as a friend and attaching a small note, stating, something like, "Hi, I'll be in (your city) in a few weeks. Would appreciate some tourist advice :) –(Your name)"

Step three is to continue the dialogue and exchange numbers. Once she agrees to be your friend and gives you some advice, continue the dialogue as we discussed earlier in this book. Given the possibility of international charges (if you're venturing overseas) or simple convenience, offer to exchange numbers with her and tell her that you two need to hang out while you are there. Keep the same wit about you. Then right before (or during) your trip, contact her and hang out! See? No more lonely walks after leaving the club, party or rave in Cancun! You now have a local girl waiting for your call!

MORE WHAT IFs

Here are some more common "what if" questions you may find yourself asking:

What if she add requests me or pokes me first?

This means she's interested or at least open to getting to know you better. If you are interested, proceed to the message exchange—don't get into a poking war!

What if she only pokes me but will not message me back?

If she only pokes you, yet ignores your messages, she's toying with you. She either has a man, is bored out of her mind, or is simply looking for you to stroke her ego. It all should mean only one thing to you: move on.

What if she flakes out on a phone call or a date, but then calls back later?

Flakey females normally have boyfriends or other guys vying for their attention. Just assume that when a female flakes, a guy who "ranked higher" than you became available and that girl picked him over you. Yet if she calls back, that usually only means that the higher-ranked guy is unavailable. So what do you do if she calls back? Make her *earn* your attention and your affection. Put her to work. And be blatant with it. Afterall, if she's using you like a spare tire, use her like a rental car.

GETTING RID OF FEMALES

So what do you do if you have a not-so-secret admirer on Facebook? How do you handle it? Well first off, try to put yourself in her position and be humble. Don't be an asshole. Yeah, I know it's annoying, but in many cases, she's just getting carried away. Here's how you give her "the hint."

Polite Approach

If she sends you a message and you know immediately that you're not romantically interested, you can reply but do *not* offer to continue the chat by asking her a question or making a suggestive comment. In other words, *don't* do what I advised in Chapter 2! Take the following example:

HER: Hi. I love your picture! Where was that taken? How are you today, cutie?

YOU: LOL, thanks. I was in Puerto Rico…great place! Enjoy your week.

In most cases, she will get the hint and keep it moving. Always be humble and diplomatic at first, even if she resembles a bullfrog.

The Brush Off Approach

So what if she doesn't leave you alone? What if you get repeatedly "poked", messaged, or wall-commented by a female? What if she just won't leave you alone after you've used the "Polite Approach?" This time, brush her off as she obviously doesn't get it. Maybe she's stubborn. Maybe she has issues. Regardless, if she was your Facebook friend, this is grounds to UN-friend her. Blocking her is another option. Simply put, do not lead a woman on if you are not interested.

The "Pay Off" Approach

This is something I've executed quite successfully and it truly works. I must give credit to New York Times Best-Selling Author, Tariq "King Flex" Nasheed for this technique. If a woman refuses to leave you alone online (or even offline), make her pay—literally! In one of King Flex's radio podcasts he discusses this method at length.[9] Make sure you check out http://www.macklessonsradio.com.

If a woman is unrelenting in her pursuit of you and ignores your previous attempts of giving her the hint, this is what you do. During her next attempt, tell her that there is something on your

---

[9] Nasheed, Tariq. "How To Get Rid Of Females." Mack Lessons Radio Show. 2007. http://www.macklessonsradio.com/index/page/3.

mind. Let her know that you need help paying a bill or that you want to buy something, yet you lack the funds. (I suggest signing up for a Paypal account which allows its users to transfer money securely and for free—therefore you won't have to see her in person for a money exchange!) In a "matter of fact" kind of way, ask for $60, $80 or even more money. Either one of two things will happen: 1). She'll fork over the money, which will at least compensate you for your time, or 2). She'll realize that dealing with you is too expensive and she'll back off. Win-win situation!

CONCLUSION

Fellas, this was not an easy book to write. Although I've met countless numbers of ladies off Facebook and other sites, it is a challenge organizing thoughts and experiences into lessons. Nonetheless, I thank each and every one of you for taking the time to read through this book!

In Chapter One, we talked about "upgrading" your profile so that females will see you in a new, alluring light. Chapter Two was about finding females and the rules to landing them. Remember to stay in your geographic region and to write a message that will grasp her attention. Chapter Three was the exhaustive breakdown, showing how to classify females from NOPE, SLOPE to POKE. Make certain that you stay around mostly POKE ladies with some SLOPE features. Chapter Four taught you how to seal the deal and quickly. You must move the interaction to the phone quickly, yet as smooth as possible! In Chapter Five, we broke down a lot of the crutches and pitfalls guys tend to run into and how to avoid them. Be careful not to message her too much, watch out for idle conversation and avoid sexual language in normal message flow!

In Chapter Six, we discussed war tactics. After getting a handle on basic "Facebook game", we taught you how to draw females in by getting them interested in replying to your actions. Chapter Seven expanded on drawing females in by providing tips on whoring yourself. Remember that part of the game is distinguishing yourself from all the other guys out there. Be different! Chapter Eight is one of my favorite chapters, as we dissected the Honesty Mackin' game. Remember to be her fantasy all the way from the website to her bedside! In Chapter Nine we discussed speed mackin' to address the needs of impatient guys, like me! Always keep interactions brief, yet meaningful enough to carry them forward! Finally, we discussed more tips to keep your mackin' mouse moving. Remember what *not* to do, how to line up females for your vacations, and finally tips on getting rid of undesirable women.

Congratulations. You are now a Facebook Datebook graduate! When you meet your first (or next) lady from Facebook, tell her that Flyness sent you! Go get 'em!

Glossary of Online
Abbreviations and Emoticons

Facebook / Internet Terminology

Wall – The location on someone's profile where you can leave public comments

Status Update – A field where you can post short updates about your whereabouts, your thoughts, and anything else that might be on your mind

Friend Request – The way to add someone into your network of friends. Once a request is approved you can see each other's profile information, in most cases.

Poke – A simple feature, which alerts someone that they've been poked. Some regard this as meaningless

Note – Another name for a message or bulletin sent via Facebook

Honesty Box – A popular Facebook application allowing users to send notes to other users, while maintaining anonymity

Pic – Photo

IM – "Instant Message"

Chat Abbreviations

lol – laughing out loud

lmao – laughing my ass off

rotflmao – rolling on the floor, laughing my ass off

smh – shaking my head

ttyl – talk to you later

wtf – what the fuck

str8 – straight

brb – be right back

w/e – whatever

ty ; tx – thank you; thanks

yw – your welcome

j/k – just kidding

For more abbreviations, visit

http://www.sharpened.net/glossary/acronyms.php

Emoticons

:) Smiley face; can also use :-)

;) Wink; sly, devious or even polite; can also use ;-)

:(Sad face; can also use :-(

:- Not satisfied; Undecided; not really "feeling it" (one of my favorites)

O:) Angel face ("I'm innocent")

For more emoticon meanings, visit
http://www.alphadictionary.com/articles/imglish/emoticons_emo
t.html

Recommended Reads

FROM MYSPACE TO MY PLACE: THE MEN'S GUIDE TO SNAGGING WOMEN ONLINE

BY YOUR ROYAL FLYNESS

FROM MYSPACE TO MY PLACE: THE LADIES' GUIDE TO FINDING MR. RIGHT OR MR. RIGHT NOW ONLINE

BY YOUR ROYAL FLYNESS

THE MACK WITHIN

BY TARIQ NASHEED

www.ingramcontent.com/pod-product-compliance
Lightning Source LLC
Chambersburg PA
CBHW051254050326
40689CB00007B/1185